SOCCER FOR MEN

About the author

Dr. Richard L. Nelson is Department Chairman and Professor of Health and Physical Education for Men at Miami University, Oxford, Ohio. He earned the B.S. in Education and the Master of Arts degrees at the Ohio State University and the Doctorate of Education degree at the University of Cincinnati.

Dr. Nelson's professional experiences include teaching at the elementary, secondary, and college levels. He was physical education and intramural director at Hamilton High School, Hamilton, Ohio, from 1953-1956. He has been teaching health and physical education at Miami University for the past nineteen years. Soccer classes are among the many activities that he has taught over the years.

As a member and officer of numerous professional organizations, Dr. Nelson has engaged in a wide variety of professional activities related to health and physical education. He has published articles concerning soccer, gymnastics, and bowling. For the past two years he has been co-director for an Ohio State Department of Education Drug and Health Education Project.

SOCCER FOR MEN

Physical Education Activities Series

Richard L. Nelson
Miami University
Oxford, Ohio

Illustrations by Milton M. Myers

Third Edition

Wm C Brown Company Publishers
Dubuque, Iowa

Consulting Editor

Aileene Lockhart
Texas Woman's University

Evaluation Materials Editor

Jane A. Mott
Smith College

Contents

Preface

The purpose of this book is to provide players with information regarding one of the world's most popular team sports—soccer. This is a vigorous game which demands skill, endurance, teamwork, and fast thinking.

These pages are not devoted merely to detailing the rules or to descriptions of *how* to perform the fundamental skills involved in soccer, although this information is included. An attempt has been made to go further; the *purpose* and *application* of skills and regulations are pointed out. In other words, it is hoped that the reader will find not only the basis for a real understanding of the sport but also may accelerate his progress and self-confidence, and, consequently, his satisfaction by applying the suggestions that are made for practice and by bearing in mind principles that will aid in the development of offensive and defensive strategy.

Self-evaluation questions are distributed throughout the text. These afford the reader typical examples of the kinds of understanding and levels of skill that he should be acquiring as he progresses toward mastery of soccer. The player should not only answer the printed questions but should pose additional ones as a self-check on learning. Since the order in which the content of the text is read and the teaching progression of the instructor are matters of individual decision, the evaluative materials are not positioned according to the presentation of given topics. In some instances the student may find that he cannot respond fully and accurately to a question until he has read more extensively or has gained more playing experience. From time to time he should return to such troublesome questions until he is sure of the answers or has developed the skills called for, as the case may be.

Instructional objectives are listed at the end of each chapter. These objectives are stated in behavioral terms; that is, they state what is to be learned and what is to be evaluated according to the content of each chapter.

Although this book is designed primarily for college men in physical education classes, the information and purposes are appropriate for all soccer players, those in high school, recreational, intramural, and interscholastic programs.

What is soccer like?

1

In contrast to most games played in the United States, soccer is played primarily with the feet. Other parts of the body, such as the head, chest, abdomen, thighs, and shins, are also brought into use in the performance of many of the basic skills. With the exception of the goalkeeper, however, the use of hands and arms is strictly prohibited.

The game is started at the halfway line within the center circle by means of a placekick. The game is played by two teams of eleven men who attempt to advance the ball toward the opponent's goal with the purpose of scoring a field goal by propelling the ball across the goal line, between the uprights, and under the crossbar.

Intercollegiate soccer rules divide a soccer game into two equal periods of forty-five minutes with a ten-minute intermission between halves. The game, as played by college classes, is usually divided into four quarters that are eight to ten minutes each with a one-minute intermission after the first and third quarters and a ten-minute intermission at the half.

The eleven players comprising a soccer team are named as follows: goalkeeper, right fullback, left fullback, right halfback, center halfback, left halfback, outside right, inside right, center forward, inside left, and outside left. Figure 1.1 shows a basic position of play for each team member.

Most American students find participation in soccer both very enjoyable and beneficial. To play the game well, one must develop physical stamina and excellent neuromuscular coordination, intellectual alertness and the abilty to make adjustments to rapidly changing situations, emotional control and gentlemanly conduct, and social graces that promote good interpersonal relationships.

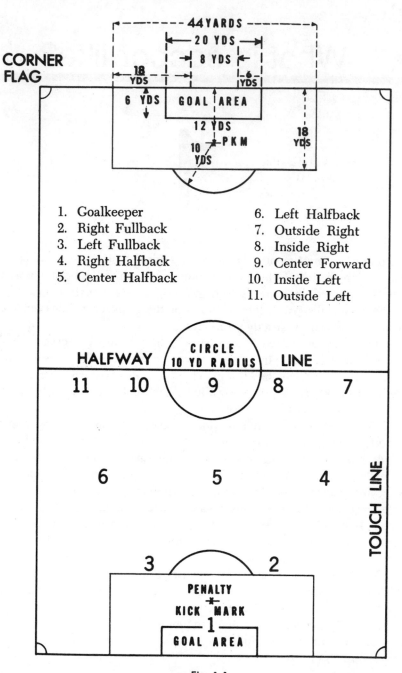

1. Goalkeeper
2. Right Fullback
3. Left Fullback
4. Right Halfback
5. Center Halfback

6. Left Halfback
7. Outside Right
8. Inside Right
9. Center Forward
10. Inside Left
11. Outside Left

Fig. 1.1

Soccer is often called the "universal game." What baseball is to the United States, soccer is to the rest of the world. It is difficult to determine how many millions of people play the game, but it is estimated that the number of fans may reach over 600 million. In many parts of the world (Europe and Latin America, for example) crowds of 100,000 or more at a single match are not uncommon. In Brazil a stadium built solely for soccer games seats 200,000 spectators! The game is played in more than 130 nations and enjoys a long history.

Within the United States, soccer has undergone tremendous growth since World War II. The game is played extensively in the East, South, Midwest, and Far West. It is played on a competitive basis in hundreds of schools, colleges, and amateur clubs. There are over seven hundred college and three thousand secondary school teams playing soccer in the United States.

As in most other sports, the skills of soccer can be practiced in an area of any size and on almost any type surface. To play the game, however, an area the size of a football field or larger is required. Within the boundaries of the official field (110 to 120 by 65 to 75 yards) are goalposts with attached nets and numerous markings, including goal areas, penalty areas, corner-kick areas, penalty marks, and a center circle (fig. 1.1).

INSTRUCTIONAL OBJECTIVES

The purpose of this chapter is to enable each student to—

1. compare and contrast soccer with other popular sports played in the United States,
2. name each player on a team and identify basic playing positions,
3. recognize the worldwide popularity of soccer,
4. explain the purpose of each of the markings on the field of play.

Skills essential for everyone

2

SKILLS AND TECHNIQUES OF KICKING

There are two groups of kicks to be mastered in soccer. The first group consists of long kicks such as the instep kick, outside of the foot kick, and volley kicks. The second group is composed of short kicks such as the push pass, lob, and flick kick.

General Information Concerning Kicking

1. Determine the direction and distance you want the ball to travel.
2. Keep your eyes on the ball at all times.
3. Learn the techniques of the kicks on a stationary or slow-moving ball.
4. Your body, especially your kicking leg, should be relaxed.
5. Use your arms to help maintain balance.
6. Practice kicking skills and techniques with both feet.
7. Long kicks generally travel distances greater than fifteen yards.

Instep Kick   The instep kick, if executed properly, will enable you to kick the ball with both power and accuracy. It can be used effectively on ground balls and bouncing balls. The instep kick is especially advantageous in scoring, free-kick, and passing situations. To perform an instep kick:

1. Place the nonkicking foot four to six inches to the side of the ball.
2. Flex the knee of the kicking foot until it blocks the ball from your view.

Place a ball on the penalty kick mark. Can you send the ball through the goalposts using a right foot instep kick? Can you do the same with your left foot? Check your accuracy from twenty, thirty, and forty yards.

3. Straighten the knee as it moves over the ball and swing the leg from the hip.

4. Keep the toe pointed down. The top portion of the foot covered by the shoelace or the inside portion of the instep should contact the ball slightly below its midpoint.

5. To keep the ball low lean forward from the waist as your foot meets the ball. Moving your arms backward and upward will help you maintain balance.

6. To loft the ball, place the nonkicking foot six to eight inches to the side of and slightly behind the ball. Lean your body backward as your foot meets the ball. Moving your arms forward and upward will help you maintain balance.

7. Follow through by continuing the upward swing of your leg (fig. 2.1).

Fig. 2.1 Instep kick

Outside of the Foot Kick   This kick is the same as the instep kick except that the toe is turned inward. It enables you to kick a fast, low curved ball with sideward spin. It is an effective means of shooting around an opponent because of the long arc which the ball travels. It is also valuable when used as a corner kick. (See instep kick for points related to the performance of this skill.)

Can you loft a ball so that it reaches your teammate at about chest level?

Volleying   The volley and half-volley kicks are executed while the ball is in the air. When executing a volley, the ball is kicked while it is in the air, either before or after it bounces (fig. 2.2). The half-volley is performed by kicking the ball just after it strikes the ground (fig. 2.3). The volley kick will yield a rather high, lofting ball, while the half-volley kick will produce a relatively low ball. To perform either:

1. Swing the kicking leg forward from the hip. Keep the knee flexed and the toe pointed down.
2. Contact the ball slightly below its midpoint with the instep or shoelace.
3. Follow through by continuing the upward swing of the leg.
4. Kick the ball while it is in the air to loft it; kick the ball near the ground to keep it low.

Fig. 2.2   Volley kick

Fig. 2.3   Half-volley kick

Inside of the Foot Kicks   The push pass and lob are excellent kicks to use for short passes and goal shots. Although these kicks are useful in maintaining control of the ball, they are not very deceptive. To perform inside of the foot kicks:

1. Swing the kicking leg forward from the hip with the knee slightly flexed and the toe pointed down and out.

2. Straighten the leg as the inside of the foot contacts the ball.
3. To perform the push pass, push the ball with the inside of the foot without causing it to bounce (fig. 2.4).
4. To perform the lob, place the inside of the foot slightly under the ball, lift your foot as you kick, and lean your body backward ((fig. 2.5).

Fig. 2.4 Push pass	**Fig. 2.5 Lob pass**

Outside of the Foot Kick   The flick or jab kick is used for short passes and dribbling. Feint movements executed before the pass is attempted make it difficult to intercept. To perform the flick kick:

1. Swing the kicking leg away from your body with the knee slightly flexed and the toe pointed down and in.
2. As the outside of the foot contacts the ball, straighten the leg.
3. Try to jab the ball with the outside of the foot and follow through with a slight outward movement of the entire leg (fig. 2.6).
4. To raise the ball off the ground, place the outside of the foot slightly under the ball and pull the ankle upward.

SKILLS AND TECHNIQUES OF CONTROL

The process of bringing the ball under your control is called trapping. Trapping is more than just stopping a ball; a trap may bring a ball to the ground,

Partners face each other about twenty yards apart. Can you pass the ball back and forth six times without losing control? Can you do the same at thirty yards? at forty yards?

Fig. 2.6   The flick kick or jab

change its direction, or slow it down. The method by which you trap the ball will be determined by your skill and also will depend upon game conditions. In general, a trap is successful when you have intercepted the ball and are ready to dribble, pass, or kick it.

General Information Concerning Trapping

1.   Keep your eyes on the ball at all times.
2.   Learn the techniques of trapping first on slow-moving balls.
3.   Maintain a relaxed body throughout the performance of the skill.

Sole of the Foot Trap   The sole of the foot can be used to trap a rolling or bouncing ball. Although this trap is simple to perform, its effectiveness is decreased as running speed is increased. To trap the ball with the sole of the foot:

1.   Extend the trapping leg forward with the foot four to five inches away from the ground and at a forty-five-degree angle to it.
2.   Allow the ball to roll into the trap formed by your foot and the ground (fig. 2.7).

Fig. 2.7   Sole of the foot trap

Side of the Foot Trap   The inside or outside of the foot may be used to deflect the ball and thereby enable you to gain control of it. This type of trap is used by all players with the exception of the goalkeeper; he would not use this trap since it would be dangerous to deflect the ball toward the goal. To trap the ball with the side of the foot:

1. Flex the knee of the trapping leg, raising the foot off the ground three to four inches.
2. Turn the foot out when deflecting the ball with the inside of the foot.
3. Turn the foot in when deflecting the ball with the outside of the foot.
4. The body should lean in the direction the ball is to go (fig. 2.8).

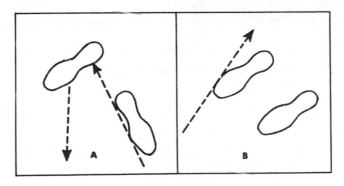

Fig. 2.8

Can you trap two out of three balls that reach you at chest height? at stomach height?

Inside of the Thigh Trap   An excellent method of gaining control of a ball in low flight is to allow it to strike the relaxed muscles of the thigh. The fleshy part of the leg absorbing the impact of the ball will cause it to drop near your feet. To trap the ball in this manner:

1. Shift your body weight to the nontrapping leg.
2. Bend the knee of the trapping leg at a right angle to the line of flight of the ball with the foot off the ground.
3. As the ball strikes the thigh, a slight backward movement of the leg from the hip will help absorb the impact and will cause the ball to drop at your feet (fig. 2.9).

Fig. 2.9   Inside of the thigh trap

Stomach and Chest Traps   These traps are used when the ball is traveling above the ground at the appropriate height, i.e., either abdomen or chest height. In either case:

1. Relax and bend forward at the waist as the ball strikes your body.
2. Extend your arms away from your body.
3. Jump off both feet and allow your body to "give" in order to absorb the impact of a hard-kicked ball.
4. Move forward in the desired direction as the ball hits your body (fig. 2.10).

Fig. 2.10   Stomach (or chest) trap

SKILLS AND TECHNIQUES OF PASSING

Passing refers to kicking the ball to a teammate. As in any other team game, good passing and pass receiving are of the utmost importance. In soccer the passer and the receiver have well-defined responsibilities. The passer must be sure he can pass the ball without its being intercepted. He should pass only to a teammate who is not marked (guarded), and he must be able to judge distances with some degree of accuracy. He also must be capable of kicking the ball with enough skill so that the receiver can gain control of it. The receiver, on the other hand, must work to be in position to receive the ball; i.e., he should move between the man marking him and the passer, he must be ready to receive a pass at all times, he must keep his eyes on the ball, and he must go to meet the ball once it is on its way toward him. Remember, a good pass is the key to team play.

Passing may be accomplished by any of the long or short kicks previously discussed. Heading (to be discussed later) may also be used as a means of passing the ball. In general, it is best to loft the ball on long passes. Game situations and weather conditions, however, will help determine when to pass the ball low or high.

General Information Concerning Passing

1.   Use a form of the instep kick for long passes.
2.   Use the inside of the foot, the outside of the foot, or the head for short passes.

Can you dribble a ball without losing control of it for twenty yards? thirty yards? fifty yards? Can you dribble a figure 8 pattern?

3. Time your pass with the speed of the receiver.
4. Devote all of your attention to your passing.

When passing:
1. Look at your receiver before kicking.
2. Look at the ball while in the act of kicking.
3. Lead the receiver; i.e., pass so that the ball will be in front of the receiver. Otherwise he will have to slow down or stop to receive the ball.
4. Use feint movements whenever possible to deceive your opponent.

SKILLS AND TECHNIQUES OF DRIBBLING

Dribbling is a method of advancing the ball by a series of short taps with the feet. The basic purpose of the dribble is to maintain possession of the ball. The dribble is used most effectively when you are not closely guarded (marked) by an opponent, when there are no unguarded teammates to whom you may pass, when you are attempting to set up a play, and when you want to maneuver for a more advantageous passing or scoring position. A simple rule to follow is to pass the ball rather than dribble whenever possible. An unnecessary dribble increases your chances of losing the ball.

General Information Concerning Dribbling

1. The ball should be kept near the feet throughout the dribble.
2. Push or tap rather than kick the ball.
3. Work for ball control rather than speed.
4. Advanced tactics such as swerving, feigning, and changing of pace make dribbling much more effective.

Inside of the Foot Dribble   This method of dribbling gives best ball control. Use the dribble only when there is no better alternative; a good pass will produce better results in your team effort to defeat an opponent. To dribble with the inside of the foot:

1. Slightly flex the knee of one leg, raising the foot three to four inches off the ground.
2. Push the ball straight ahead with the inside of your foot.

Can you throw the ball two out of three times to the feet of a teammate ten yards away? fifteen yards?

3. Keep your body forward and keep your head over the ball.
4. Step forward, shifting the body weight to the dribbling leg, and repeat the movements with the other foot (fig. 2.11).

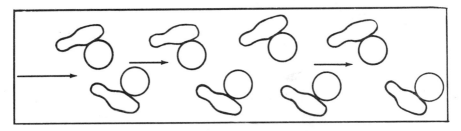

Fig. 2.11   Inside of the foot dribble

SKILLS AND TECHNIQUES OF THROWING IN

The technique of the throw-in is governed basically by the throw-in rule. The thrower must face the field of play and must have part of each foot either on the touchline or on the ground outside the touchline at the moment of delivering the ball. He must use both hands and must deliver the ball from over his head.

The throw-in is important not only because it is a method of restarting play, but also because it is a way of initiating offensive play.

General Information Concerning Throwing In

1. Assume a comfortable, balanced stance with the feet either slightly apart or one foot ahead of the other. A few running steps may be taken if desired.
2. Try to conceal the direction of the throw until the last moment.
3. Lead the receiver; i.e., throw the ball so that it will be in front of him.

Throwing with One Foot in Advance of the Other   This method has the advantage of enabling the thrower to bend his body backwards and maintain balance. Consequently, a more powerful throw can be executed due to the longer forward sweep of the trunk and arms. As with any method of delivering the throw, care must be taken to keep a portion of both feet on the ground.

Can you head two out of three balls a distance of five yards to the feet of a teammate? four out of five balls?

1. Place your hands on opposite sides of the ball with the fingers comfortably spread.
2. Place one foot approximately four to six inches ahead of the other.
3. As you shift your body weight to the rear leg, take the ball over and well behind your head and bend your body backwards. Keep the heels slightly off the ground. (fig. 2.12).
4. As you initiate the throw, transfer your weight from the rear leg to the front leg.
5. The wrists, elbows, shoulders, and trunk muscles are used in executing the throw.
6. Follow through by extending the arms, wrists, and fingers forward in front of the body.

Fig. 2.12 Throwing with one foot in advance of the other

SKILLS AND TECHNIQUES OF HEADING

The skill of heading consists of bringing the ball under control by means of the head. Thus, when you use your head physically, you are also using it mentally. Heading can be used as a method of passing the ball, scoring a goal, or bringing the ball to the ground.

For reasons of safety, a number of factors must be kept in mind when heading. First, you cannot push off or climb up an opponent for the purpose of heading. Second, you should never charge an opponent while he is in the air heading the ball. Third, you should never create a "dangerous play" by heading a ball lower than waist height. (Similarly, you should never kick at a ball higher than shoulder height.)

General Information Concerning Heading

1. The best type of heading directs the ball to the ground (to your feet or a teammate's feet).
2. Use your entire upper body to obtain speed and power.
3. Keep your eyes on the ball until it meets your forehead.
4. Keep your eyes open throughout the performance of the skill.
5. Jump up to meet the ball.

To head the ball:

1. Jump off the ground in order to meet the ball in the air.
2. While in the air use your arms to maintain balance.
3. Bend your body backward at the waist and use your neck muscles to direct the ball forcefully to the ground.
4. The midpoint of the ball should make contact with your forehead at the hairline.
5. Stiffen your neck and throw your head at the ball.
6. To head the ball to the side, meet the ball with the side of your forehead and thrust your head to the side (fig. 2.13).

Fig. 2.13   Heading the ball

Can you repeatedly head the ball fifteen to eighteen inches above your head so that it remains airborne? Can you keep the ball airborne by using your feet and your head?

SKILLS AND TECHNIQUES OF CHARGING AND TACKLING

Charging is a method of unbalancing your opponent when he has possession, or is attempting to secure possession, of the ball. A fair charge consists of a nudge or a contact with your near shoulder. When charging, both players must be in an upright position and within playing distance of the ball. In addition, both players must have at least one foot on the ground and their arms held close to their bodies. The charge must not be violent and cannot be made from behind unless your opponent is intentionally obstructing.

Tackling is a method of gaining possession of the ball by use of the feet. A tackle is also considered successful if you force the dribbler to make a poor pass or otherwise interfere with his control of the ball. More often than not, tackling and charging are used in concert.

General Information Concerning Charging and Tackling

1. Watch your opponent for swerving and feint tactics and recognize these for what they are: attempts to fool you.
2. Do not charge and tackle until your opponent has moved in a given direction with the ball.
3. Do not charge violently; govern the force of the charge according to the speed at which you and your opponent are traveling.
4. Make every attempt to gain possession of the ball rather than just "bumping" your opponent.

One-Leg Tackle   This type of tackle is used head on, from the side, or from the rear. To tackle an approaching opponent with one leg:

1. Nudge your opponent's shoulder with your right shoulder and place the inside of your right foot against the ball (fig. 2.14).
2. Trap the ball with your right foot and leg.
3. Push the ball forward with your right foot and step forward with your left leg.
4. Perform the sole of the foot tackle by trapping the ball between your foot and the ground.

Fig. 2.14   Charging and Tackling

5. Perform the two-leg tackle by placing both feet in front of the ball with the heels close together. Turn your knees outward and lean your body forward. Trap the ball between your legs as the shoulder charge is made.

INSTRUCTIONAL OBJECTIVES

The purpose of this chapter is to enable each student to—

1. identify general principles that apply to learning each of the basic skills of soccer,
2. synthesize information pertaining to the proper execution of each of the basic skills,
3. analyze the game situations in which each of the basic skills may be useful.

Better players master
these techniques

3

Whether or not you are ready for the following skills, you should know what they are, when they are used, and be able to appreciate skilled play when you see it.

ADDITIONAL KICKING SKILLS

Pivot Instep Kick   The pivot instep kick has the distinct advantage of enabling you to change the direction of the ball. In essence, the ball will travel at right angles to your approach. This kick is used on ground balls only; it is particularly effective for corner kicks and in scoring situations. To perform a pivot instep kick:

1. Place the nonkicking foot no more the eighteen inches behind and slightly to the inside of the ball.
2. Swing the kicking leg forward from the hip, keeping the knee slightly flexed and the toe pointed down.
3. Pivot on the nonkicking foot as the kicking leg swings forward.
4. Contact the ball slightly below its midpoint with the shoelace.
5. Follow through by continuing the upward swing of the leg (fig. 3.1).
6. Lean forward and work for forward spin on the ball in order to keep the ball low.

Sole of Foot and Heel Kicks   In general, these kicks are difficult for beginners in soccer. Nevertheless, they are good backward passes and provide

Can you kick two out of three goals from a distance of fifteen yards using the pivot instep kick to kick a stationary ball? a moving ball?

Fig. 3.1   Pivot instep kick

a means of stopping a rolling ball. In executing both kicks, it is essential that you know where you are passing. These kicks are more difficult if the ball is rolling and you are running. Practice and good judgment will eliminate stepping on the ball. To succeed with these kicks:

1. Place the nonkicking foot to the side of the ball.
2. Keep the knee of the kicking foot flexed until the ball is under your body.
3. To execute the sole of the foot kick, place the sole of the foot lightly on the ball and kick the ball behind you by flexing the knee (fig. 3.2).
4. To execute the heel kick, hit the ball in the center with your heel as you swing the leg backward from the hip (fig. 3.3).

ADDITIONAL DRIBBLING SKILLS

Outside of Foot Dribble   This type of dribbling is used when attempting to keep your body between an opponent and the ball. The ball is dribbled with the same foot every other step. Although this method of dribbling gives greater speed, it is difficult to execute and decreases ball control. To dribble with the outside of the foot:

1. Slightly flex the knee of one leg, raising the foot three to four inches off the ground.

Is A, B, or C the best position from which to tackle the dribbler? How might the dribbler evade the tackler?

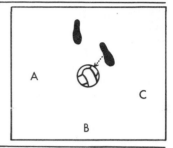

Fig. 3.2   Sole of the foot kick

Fig. 3.3   Heel kick

2. Push the ball straight ahead with the outside of the foot.
3. Keep the body weight forward with the head over the ball.
4. Step forward, shifting the body weight to the dribbling leg. Continue the forward motion by stepping through with the opposite leg, repeating the movements with the dribbling leg (fig. 3.4).

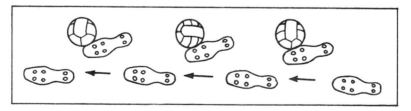

Fig. 3.4   Outside of the foot dribble

Side of Foot Volley   This type of volley is used for short accurate kicks and for maintaining control of the ball. It is used when the ball is approximately knee-high or lower. To perform the side of the foot volley:

1. Flex the kicking leg at the hip and the knee so that the knee points sideward and the foot turns outward.
2. Swing the kicking leg forward from the hip.
3. Contact the ball slightly below its midpoint with the side of the foot (fig. 3.5).
4. Follow through by continuing the forward swing of the leg.

Fig. 3.5   Side of foot volley

ADDITIONAL TACKLING SKILLS

Sliding Tackle   This is a difficult skill to perform and can lead to a dangerous play situation if it is executed improperly. Beginning and intermediate players should not attempt to hook the ball away from a dribbler in this manner since it is dangerous. Moreover, it forces the tackler to the ground and eliminates him from further play on the ball. To perform the sliding tackle:

1. Initiate the slide to the ground by flexing the knee of the leg closest to the ground (fig. 3.6).
2. Contact the ground with the leg, thigh, and/or buttock.
3. Maintain balance by placing the hand on the sliding side of the body on the ground. Keep your elbow flexed.

Fig. 3.6   Sliding tackle

4. Extend the takeoff leg forward toward the ball in an attempt to hook it with the instep of the foot (fig. 3.6).

INSTRUCTIONAL OBJECTIVES

The purpose of this chapter is to enable each student to—

1. recognize advanced soccer skills and examine their purposes and execution,
2. analyze the game situations in which each of the advanced skills may be useful.

Progress can be speeded up

4

Learning is a complex process. Nevertheless, there are ways to facilitate your learning of motor skills. At this point you are probably asking yourself this question: "How can I possibly remember to use all the information related to the performance and strategy of soccer?" Experience has shown that you will learn more easily and remember longer if you learn with understanding. In other words, you must not only learn the "how" of motor skills, but also the "why" and "when." As you no doubt observed in the preceding chapters, the material in this booklet is organized so that you will develop understanding. Each major technique is introduced by giving you general information that provides the specific points essential to learning the skill. Before each skill is broken down into its major components, however, its purpose and its application in game situations are discussed.

HOW TO PRACTICE

It is important to realize at the outset that if you wish to become proficient at the game of soccer, you must want to learn. There is no single aspect of learning more important than your attitude toward the game. It is a well-proved statement that practice in and of itself does not make perfect. Practice of correct movements, of course, is basic, but perfection depends upon more than mere repetition. What does lead to perfection, then, is purposiveness of practice or repetition that is active and highly motivated.

Place an obstacle at each corner of a twenty-foot square. Can you dribble around the perimeter in twenty-seven seconds or less?

Hints for Learning

You no doubt will find the game of soccer enjoyable as you improve old skills and learn new ones. Soccer, like all other team games, requires basic skills, knowledge, and understanding that must be individually mastered and then applied to game situations in connection with teamwork. As in all learning situations, what you get out of class instruction depends entirely on you. You must be receptive to new ideas and attempt new things even though they may be different or difficult at first. You must be willing to apply yourself in learning knowledge and skills. Only through practice of basic movements beyond the point of bare mastery will you step out of the beginner's class. You must be willing to accept constructive criticism with the intention of correcting errors and misunderstandings as you become aware of them.

Check yourself on the following points to determine your progress in skill performance and team proficiency:

1. Do I understand the explanations and demonstrations of basic skills and strategies so that I have a *mental picture* of their execution?
2. Do I understand the purpose and application of skills and strategies in game situations?
3. Have I practiced the skills and strategies both as an individual and as a member of a small group?
4. Am I open to suggestions and corrections in learning situations?
5. Do I attempt to use new learning in game situations?

If the answers to the questions are in the affirmative, you are well on your way to improvement and success in the game of soccer.

Practice Formations for Large Classes

Since soccer is a team game, it is logical that much of your practice should be in groups. There should be at least one ball for every eight men. The following drills are designed for eight or more men. The player with the ball is designated by B; the path of the ball is represented by ----; the path of the player is represented by ----; a player in formation is designated by O.

Double Column   This formation is used for kicks, passes, trapping, and heading. The players in each line are spaced approximately four yards apart;

From a stationary position with the legs spread approximately fifteen to eighteen inches apart, can you smoothly tap a ball back and forth from foot to foot and keep the ball on the ground? Can you alternate the speed of the ball from slow to fast and back to slow again?

the two columns are spaced approximately ten yards apart; for long kicks the two columns are spaced approximately twenty yards apart (fig. 4.1).

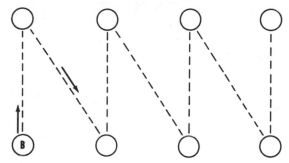

Fig. 4.1   Double column formation

Single Column   The players are spaced five yards apart in a column. One player with the ball stands in front of and faces the other players. The player with the ball dribbles in and out around the other players. As skill in dribbling is gained, the players in the column may attempt to steal the ball but must keep one foot stationary (fig. 4.2).

Fig. 4.2   Single column formation

Divided Column   The column is divided in half. Players line up in single file, each column facing the other. The player with the ball kicks it to the first player opposite him and goes to the end of the line. The player receiving the ball traps it, returns the ball by means of a kick, and goes to the end of the line, etc. (fig. 4.3).

Fig. 4.3   Divided column formation

Semicircle and Circle   The players form a semicircle twelve to fifteen yards in front of the goal. If a goalkeeper is used, he can practice goalkeeper skills while the players in the semicircle practice goal shooting. Several balls can be used if kicked one after the other, not simultaneously (fig. 4.4).

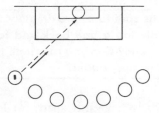

Fig. 4.4   Semicircle formation

The players are spaced approximately five yards apart forming a circle. The player in the middle throws the ball to a player in the circle who heads it back, etc. The ball should be thrown fifteen to twenty feet into the air (fig. 4.5).

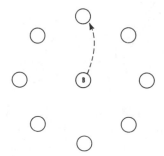

Fig. 4.5   Circle formation

Field Drills   One or two examples of field drills should enable your team to understand their organization and purpose and to devise other such drills as needed (figs. 4.6 and 4.7).

Activities for Large Groups

Many enjoyable lead-up games afford opportunities for practicing game skills and strategies. Since many of these games are relatively simple in organization, only brief descriptions of them are given.

Soccer Dodge Ball   This game is played in the same manner as regular dodge ball except that the ball must be kicked.

Circle Keep Away   The players in the circle attempt to keep the ball away from the player in the center. The arms and hands cannot be used.

Soccer Steal the Bacon   The game is played in the same manner as regular "steal the bacon" except that the ball must be dribbled.

Line Soccer   The players form two lines approximately twenty yards apart. Each line of players is assigned a number. The instructor, or an ap-

Rotate from 1 to 2, 2 to 3, 3 to 4, etc.

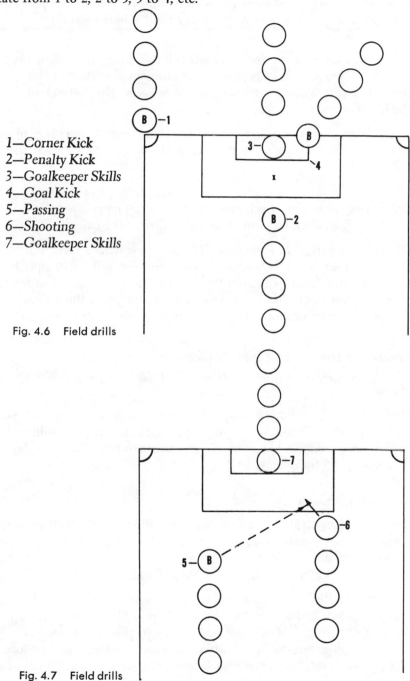

1—*Corner Kick*
2—*Penalty Kick*
3—*Goalkeeper Skills*
4—*Goal Kick*
5—*Passing*
6—*Shooting*
7—*Goalkeeper Skills*

Fig. 4.6   Field drills

Fig. 4.7   Field drills

Can you kick two out of three goals from a distance of fifteen yards using the pivot instep kick to kick a stationary ball? a moving ball?

pointed leader, rolls the ball between the two lines and calls a player or players by number. Those players whose numbers are called run out to play the ball. The remaining players act as goalkeepers. The ball cannot go over the heads of the line players.

Circle Play   The players form a circle approximately ten yards in diameter. The object of the game is to keep the ball in the air by heading or volleying it.

Dribbling Relay   One group forms a line with players spaced approximately five yards apart. Each player in the remaining group dribbles in and out of the line, attempting to maintain control of the ball.

Offensive-Defensive Situations   There are numerous variations of this activity: one-on-one situation where one offensive player attempts to outmaneuver one defensive player; two-on-one situation where two offensive players attempt to outmaneuver one defensive player; a three-on-two situation where three offensive players attempt to outmanuver two defensive players.

Rotation Soccer   This game is played as regular soccer with the exception that the players rotate to different positions after a specified length of of time.

Half Field Play   Each team plays on one half of the field. Five players assume forward positions, and six players assume halfback, fullback, and goalkeeper positions. The forwards remain on offense for five plays and then change to the defense.

Activities for Small Groups

There are many small group activities that will enable students to simulate game conditions more realistically. Only a few of those activities are included here. The student will find it interesting and helpful to design additional activities that will benefit himself and his team.

Two-on-Two Play   Only a section of the field is used and boundaries of play are established within that section. The drill can be changed by indicating dribbling, passing, shooting, offensive play, defensive play, heading, or trapping. For example, within one-quarter of the field, two forwards play against one fullback and a goalkeeper, or within the width of the goal area from the goal line to midfield two defensive players attempt to stop two offensive players.

Three-on-Three Play   Only a section of the field is used and boundaries of play are established within that section. The drill can be changed by indicating dribbling, passing, shooting, defensive play, offensive play, heading, or trapping. For example, within one-third of the field three forwards attempt to score against two fullbacks and a goalie, or within one-half of the field three offensive players attempt to outmaneuver three defensive players.

Accuracy Drills   Place two players or one player and a marker fifteen yards apart. The object of the drill is to propel the ball to a given player, through the goal, or to a given area by means of a pass, a throw-in, a head, or a kick.

Heading Drill   Place three markers ten to fifteen yards from the touchline. Player A stands near the touchline while Player B lobs the ball into the air and calls a target number. Player A attempts to head the ball to the selected target.

Kicking Drill   This drill is especially good for goalkeepers, fullbacks, and halfbacks. Place two teams consisting of three players each on opposite touchlines. Team A kicks the ball to Team B. Team B returns the kick from where the ball strikes the ground. The team that advances the ball over the touchline first is the winner.

Shooting Drill   Place two soccer balls two to three yards apart and about fifteen yards from the goal. One player attempts to score by shooting one ball at the goal. He then shoots the second ball as quickly as possible. As skill increases, another player can roll one ball toward the shooter. The shot must then be executed on the run while the ball is moving.

Three-Man Weave   Three players form a line ready to move downfield. The middle man starts play by passing the ball to one of the other players. He then cuts behind the man to whom he passes. The man who receives the ball passes to the third player and cuts behind him. This pattern is continued throughout the drill.

Chip-Shot Drill   Three men form a triangle ready to move downfield. Player A passes the ball forward to Player B who passes the ball to Player C. Player C chips the ball over Player B's head to Player A who has moved further downfield.

Pass and Go   Three men form a triangle. Player A passes to Player B and follows his pass to assume Player B's position. Player B passes to Player C

Can you approach a stationary ball at a moderate run and then pass it backward to a teammate who is standing five yards behind the ball? As you dribble the ball, can you pass it backward to a teammate who is following you?

and follows his pass to assume Player C's position. This pattern is continued throughout the drill.

CONDITIONING EXERCISES

It is essential that you develop physical strength and endurance to play the game of soccer well. Strength can be defined best as the ability of the whole body or a part of the body to apply force. By increasing strength, it is then possible to increase muscular power that is a combination of strength and speed. Endurance can be defined as the ability of the entire body or a part of the body to resist fatigue and to recover quickly after fatigue occurs. When you can maintain a given level of performance for longer periods of time, you are achieving a higher level of endurance.

The average physical education class meets for two or three one-hour periods per week. Most class time must be spent learning about the game and practicing skills and strategies. Therefore, the student who desires a higher level of conditioning than is possible through class participation must engage in additional activities outside of the classroom.

The only way to increase strength and endurance is by means of the *overload principle*. Overload for strength means that muscles must be "loaded" by increasing the resistance or stress beyond previous requirements. Overload for endurance means that the muscle group or the total body must be worked beyond previous repetition levels.

A detailed, technical discussion of muscular effectiveness cannot be presented here. Information concerning these matters can be found in current books and journals. A few conditioning exercises are briefly explained, however. These exercises can be performed in or out of class and will, for the most part, increase both strength and endurance.

General Exercises

1. Vigorous performance in sports and games.
2. Exercises in which the body weight is the resistance, for example, pull-ups, dips, rope climbing, and hanging-type activities.
3. Weight training equipment, including barbells, the Universal weight machine, and the Nautilus weight machine.

4. Isometric exercises in which there is muscular tension against a fixed object or another part of the body.
5. Interval training that involves a series of short periods (thirty to sixty seconds) of vigorous exercise with a short period (two or three minutes) of rest or light exercise between each work period.
6. Running on level ground and cross-country.
7. Calisthenics involving running in place, hopping, arm swinging, leg swinging, jumping, leg stretching, trunk rotation, trunk flexion, push-ups, sit-ups, leg lifts, and leg abduction and adduction.
8. Ball exercises that involve the skills and strategies of the game.

Specific Exercises

1. *Neck Flexion.*   Lie on your back and bring your chin to your chest while someone applies a downward pressure at your forehead.
2. *Neck Extension and Hyperextension.*   Lie face down and raise your head as far as possible while someone applies a downward pressure at the back of your head.
3. *Trunk Rotation.*   Sit on the ground with your hands placed behind your head. Twist to one side as far as possible while someone applies a resisting pressure at your upper arms.
4. *Trunk Extension and Hyperextension.*   Lie face down with your hands at the small of your back. Raise your head and trunk as far as possible while someone holds your feet down.
5. *Hip Flexion.*   Sit on the edge of a table. Be sure that your leg is supported from the hip to the knee. Raise your thigh while someone applies a downward pressure at the knee.
6. *Hip Extension.*   Rest the upper part of your body on a table with your face down. Hold the sides of the table and raise one leg with the knee straight while someone applies a downward pressure at the knee. Try this with pressure applied at the heel.
7. *Hip Adduction.*   Lie on your back with your legs spread. Bring your legs together while someone applies outward pressure on the lower part of the legs.
8. *Hip Abduction.*   Lie on your back with your legs together. Spread your legs apart while someone applies inward pressure on the lower part of the legs.
9. *Knee Extension.*   Sit on the edge of a table. Be sure that your legs are supported from the hip to the knee. Raise your foot until your leg

is fully extended while someone applies a downward pressure at the ankle.

10. *Knee Flexion.*   Lie face down and flex your leg at the knee while someone applies a downward pressure at the ankle.

DETERMINING INSTRUCTIONAL GROUPS

Grouping students for instructional purposes is an important part of teaching physical activities. Generally, at the beginning of a soccer unit there is little time for elaborate skill-testing procedures. Most classes will have beginner, intermediate, and advanced skill levels. The instructor can utilize his time best and make the class more interesting and meaningful if he groups students into these general categories for class instruction.

Possibly, the quickest way to place students in instructional groups is by means of a short, objective test. Ten to fifteen questions concerning soccer rules, skills, and strategies provide considerable information about students' backgrounds in soccer. This technique, coupled with a simple classification of skill by which the student indicates his personal judgment about his skill and knowledge of soccer, is an effective means of establishing initial instructional groups. A classification scale such as the one included here can be used.

—— Beginner   He knows very little about soccer and has never received instruction or played the game.

—— Intermediate   He knows a little about soccer through previous instruction and class participation.

—— Advanced   He plays soccer on a regular basis and/or has played on competitive teams.

Skill-Test Items

If time permits, more elaborate skill-test items may be employed. Only brief descriptions of the skill test are included here. In each instance distribute the high ability players equally among the various teams or squads.

Obstacle Run   Time each class member as he runs an obstacle course. The obstacles may be chairs, wooden stands, hurdles (both high and low), side horses, and so on.

Kicking for Distance and/or Accuracy   Measure the distance each class member can kick the ball when he uses a specified soccer kick. If accuracy is the primary objective, allow each class member three specified soccer kicks to another player or to a predetermined area.

Throwing for Distance and Accuracy   Measure the distance each class member can throw the ball by using a throw-in or any other type of throw used by the goalkeeper. If accuracy is the primary objective, allow each class member three specified throws to another player or to a predetermined area.

Sprinting   Time each class member as he runs the twenty-five, fifty, or seventy-five yard dash.

Standing Long Jump   Measure the distance each class member can jump from a standing, two-foot takeoff.

Potato Race   Place two boxes fifteen yards apart with two tennis balls in the first box. The player reaches into the first box, secures one tennis ball, runs to the box fifteen yards away, and deposits the tennis ball into that box. He then runs back to the first box, retrieves the second ball, returns to the second box to deposit it, and then finishes when he steps past the first box.

BASIC SAFETY CONSIDERATIONS

One of the primary responsibilities of an instructor is the health and safety of class members. Each class period should be well organized, properly instructed, and adequately supervised during practice and game situations. Students, of course, must also assume their share of the responsibility for the health and safety of themselves and other class members. If the instructor and the students are aware of the potential hazards that can occur in a vigorous, running game such as soccer, many accidents and injuries can be avoided.

1. Select a field that is the appropriate size and is free from obstructions on or holes in the area of play.
2. Provide proper class organization, instruction, and supervision.
3. Provide proper conditioning of class members prior to vigorous activity.
4. Allow time for warming up during the first few minutes of each class.
5. Stress the proper execution of skills and a basic knowledge of game rules.
6. Provide adequate officiating in game situations.
7. Do not allow horseplay of any kind in class.
8. During game situations watch for undue fatigue.
9. Avoid fast-moving drills and games on rainy days.
10. Make provisions for the treatment of minor cuts, bruises, and blisters.

INSTRUCTIONAL OBJECTIVES

The purpose of this chapter is to enable each student to—

1. examine factors that can affect learning and explore ways to facilitate the learning of skills and knowledge,
2. identify basic instructional formations and activities for both large and small groups and describe their uses in the learning situation,
3. devise a conditioning program that will improve strength and endurance,
4. conclude that personal health and safety are important results of class instruction and participation.

Patterns of Play

5

For a team to be effective, each player must assume responsibility for the position he plays. Moreover, each player must be aware of the positions and responsibilities of his teammates. Only through such a thorough knowledge of the game and through mutual cooperation can team members avoid working at cross-purposes.

THE TWO-BACK SYSTEM

The following discussion concerning players and their positions is based on the 2-3-5 system or the two-back game. Although this system is old, it is quite effective with beginners. Since beginners in soccer lack advanced skills and maneuvers and have not yet learned intricate offenses, they are able to play and enjoy the two-back game without taking undue advantage of only two defensive men.

After players become proficient in skills and maneuvers and gain the necessary understanding of soccer, they should be introduced to the three- or four-back game. Brief discussions of these systems are presented later in the chapter.

The Goalkeeper

The goalkeeper should be physically agile and mentally alert. Generally, a skilled basketball player who has good height and reach possesses the necessary qualifications.

On a goal kick, where should X (defending team) send the ball? What
should his teammates, Y and Z, do?

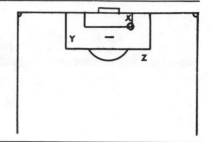

The goalkeeper constitutes the last stage of defense and the first stage of offense. Thus, his job is not only to keep the opponent from scoring but also to clear the ball from the goal area. His primary position of play is within the penalty area (fig. 5.1). He should assumed a well-balanced stance, two or three paces in front of the goal line, facing the ball When attempting to pick up a potential scorer, he should advance to reduce the angle of the shot, being careful not to let the scorer get inside the goal area with the ball. It is evident, then, that a considerable amount of play by the goalkeeper will occur outside the goal area but within the penalty area. Although the goalkeeper may play the ball outside the penalty area, he may not touch the ball with his hands outside this area. Common sense and good goaltending suggest that he remain within the penalty area when possible.

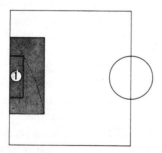

Fig. 5.1 Area of play
for goalkeeper

The goalkeeper's greatest advantage over his opponent is the fact that he can use his hands. He should be skillful in fielding, tipping, punching, striking, and diving for the ball. When fielding a rolling ball, he should bend at the knees and waist, keeping his heels together. He should place one knee on the ground to retrieve a bouncing ball. If the ball is in the air, he should get it to his chest as soon as possible and move to either side of the goal. Tipping the ball refers to placing the hand under the ball, thus causing it to go over the crossbar. Punching and striking are accomplished by hitting the ball with the fist to change its direction. Diving for the ball, i.e., leaving the ground in an effort to reach the ball, is not a wise maneuver for the in-experienced goalie since keeping or returning to a proper defensive position is difficult. While this ability is sometimes necessary, it should be used only as a last resort.

If the goalkeeper has sufficient time to catch the ball rather than de-flect it, he must decide on a plan of action for clearing it. Regardless of the method of clearing the ball, he should move to either side of the goal area first. Experience has proved that a long, accurate throw to a teammate is most successful. If a kick is to be used, however, either a punt or half-volley is effective. The half-volley has a decided advantage because it yields dis-tance without achieving excessive height.

An inexperienced goalkeeper should be extremely careful about leaving the goal ungarded when he does not have the ball. In general, he should leave the net only in a desperation charge at a dribbler or in an attempt to get to the ball before anyone else does.

The goalkeeper's position of play affords him the best opportunity of directing the defense, especially the fullbacks and halfbacks. Cooperative efforts between the goalkeeper and the backs will develop better individual play and will improve defensive strategy.

The Fullbacks

The right and left fullbacks are basically defensive players. They must have the ability to size up situations correctly and quickly; they must be alert and aggressive. The primary position of play for each fullback is approximately a quarter section of his half of the field (fig. 5.2). Each fullback, however, in many game situations will extend his area of play to include the entire penalty area to the middle of the field. The fullbacks should seldom, if ever, cross the halfway line and leave the goal area unprotected.

The two fullbacks should be in staggered position at all times. Each player marks the outside forward on his side of the field. When one fullback

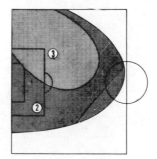

Fig. 5.2   Area of play
for left fullback

has moved out to play the ball or tackle an opponent, the other fullback must move to the middle of the field to afford adequate cover. These two players must not only work together but must also be alert to directions from the goalkeeper. Above all, they must not crowd the goalkeeper or interfere with his play. One of the fullbacks should be ready to move into the goal area if the goalkeeper is forced to leave the goal unprotected. It must be remembered, however, that the fullback cannot touch the ball with his hands.

Fullbacks should possess the ability to kick the ball with either foot. The major objective of the fullbacks is to clear the ball to a teammate if possible. The accomplishment of this objective may necessitate kicking the ball to the goalkeeper or to any other teammate who is not being closely marked. It may mean kicking the ball out-of-bounds under a pressed attack. The two most useful kicks for fullbacks are the volley and half-volley. Two particularly dangerous situations that fullbacks should avoid are dribbling and passing in front of the goal. Obviously, these tactics should be employed only when there is adequate space and time, conditions seldom enjoyed by fullbacks.

The Halfbacks

The center half and the right and left halfbacks form the backbone of the soccer team. As key players they must be fast, energetic, and in especially good physical condition. They also must possess skill in kicking, heading, and tackling. Each of these positions requires alert defensive and offensive play.

The position of play for the center half is the middle of the field, between the right and left halfbacks. He is responsible for that portion of the field extending from his own goal area to the opponent's penalty area (fig. 5.3). On defense the center half marks the opposing center forward and attempts to stop any down-the-middle attack. On offense he attempts to pass the ball ahead to his own forwards.

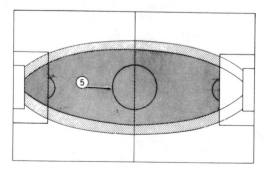

Fig. 5.3 Area of play for center halfback

The central position of the center half affords him the opportunity to direct the attack. Although he will attempt to score occasionally, he will lob the ball into the penalty area so others can try for a goal in most instances.

The position of play for the halfbacks can be understood best by looking at figure 5.4. As can be seen, the halfback should seldom advance more than three-fourths of the length of the field. In other words, he must avoid going too far up field in the attack and thereby neglecting his defensive duties.

Defensively, the halfback usually marks the inside forward on his side of the field. There will be times, however, when it will be necessary for him to mark the outside forward or the center forward. In all cases he should force the dribbler to the outside of the field.

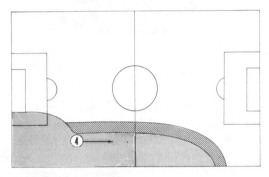

Fig. 5.4   Area of play
for right halfback

Offensively, the halfback provides support for the forward line. His ability to pass the ball accurately sets the stage for the attack. Since the halfback is usually responsible for throw-ins, he should develop the ability to throw the ball accurately.

The Forwards

The center forward, the inside right, the inside left, the outside right, and the outside left form the forward line of a soccer team. Since these players carry the attack deep into the opponent's territory, they have many opportunities to score goals. In order that they can carry out their assignments effectively, both offensively and defensively, they must possess skill, stamina, speed, and general fitness.

Ideally, the center forward should be above average in size, skill, and speed. His size should permit him to charge and tackle heavier opponents. He should be well versed in heading, kicking, turning, and passing with either foot. He should have the ability to move about quickly so that he can receive passes, execute passes, mark the opposing center half, or harass the opposing backs as the situation may warrant.

The center forward is first and foremost, however, an offensive player. He is often referred to as an "opportunist." Although he will shoot many times and score many goals, it is important for him to look for opportunities to pass to the inside forwards or outside forwards when he is closely marked. By playing a waiting game, he provides an excellent decoy and is fresh when the attack gets underway. His position of play is the middle of the field in an area from the center circle to the opponent's goal area (fig. 5.5).

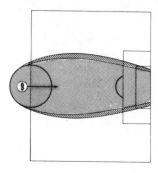

Fig. 5.5   Area of play
for center forward

The right and left inside forwards do not require the speed of outside forwards, but they must have the ability of work tirelessly. Offensively, the inside forward acts in the capacity of a playmaker. He may be able to draw the opponent out of position by means of a dribble or work the ball to a teammate who is not closely marked by means of an accurate pass. The tactic of switching positions with the outside forward after passing to him will help to confuse the opponent. Frequently a long, accurate pass to the far outside forward will set up a scoring situation on the weak side. A valuable maneuver for one of the inside forwards is that of following up attempted goal shots in an effort to get a second try for a goal.

The position of play for the inside forwards can be readily observed in figure 5.6. As indicated, the inside forwards narrow their area of play as they approach the penalty area. It should be noted that these players must avoid going too far upfield in the attack, for if they do they will necessarily neglect their defensive duties.

Defensively, the inside forward must mark the opposing halfback, assist his own halfbacks in stopping offensive moves down the field, and cover the opposing inside forward on throw-ins taken by the opponents.

The outside forward positions call for players who have speed and skill in passing, dribbling, and ball control. Insofar as speed is concerned, the outside forwards must be able to stay with or ahead of the ball at all times. Also, they must be able to outmaneuver their opponents if they are to be effective during the attack.

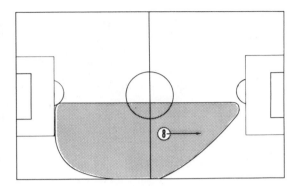

Fig. 5.6   Area of play
for inside right

The ability to kick long, accurate passes at the proper time is an important part of outside forward play. Even though the outside forwards shoot on occasions and sometimes score many goals, they should constantly watch for opportunities to center the ball to the center forward or cross the ball to the opposite inside forward or outside forward. In addition to long passes, the outside forwards execute many short passes in their cooperative efforts with the inside forwards and halfbacks.

The touchline on one side of the outside forwards and the opponent on the opposite side limit their areas of play. Under these conditions, dribbling can be used to advantage. A well-executed dribble can be used to draw the opponent out of position or from in front of the goal before passing to a teammate. The ability to receive passes on the run from any direction and to maintain control of the ball will enable the outside forwards to dribble, pass, or shoot to a distinct advantage.

The position of play for the outside forwards is shown in figure 5.7. Normally the outside forwards play six or seven yards in from the touchline; however, they must be ready to move toward the goal area when the situation warrants it. Generally the outside forwards kick all corner kicks. Game con-

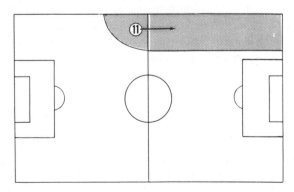

Fig. 5.7   Area of play
for outside left

As a general rule, is it best for the defending team to send this throw to teammate A, B, or C? Why?

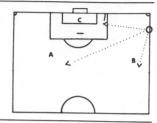

ditions will govern placement of the corner kick. On throw-ins by the opponent, the outside forward should cover the fullback opposed to him.

THE THREE-BACK SYSTEM

It might be wise to point out that limited class time, large class enrollments, and even limited facilities and equipment may not permit a thorough coverage of all the systems of the game of soccer. Be that as it may, the third-man-back game is quite popular in competitive soccer and could be taught to intermediate or advanced soccer players.

If the center halfback plays as the third back between his two fullbacks, one of his major responsibilities is that of defense; it is his job to cover the middle area in front of the goal and stop the down-the-middle attack. The center half then, in his role as defender, should seldom, if ever, cross the halfway line.

The loss of the center halfback on offense will, of necessity, increase the area to be covered by the right and left halfbacks. They must widen and extend their area of play to approximately the entire length and one-half the width of the field so that there is adequate coverage.

Similarly, the area of play for the forwards will change somewhat. The inside forwards should cover approximately one-half the field from their own penalty area to the opposing goal box. The outside forwards should come back farther and widen their area of play so that they cover approximately three-fourths the length and one-half the width of the field.

This system has the advantage of having three backs on defense. It is an effective defense against the W offense; however, it is ineffective in the face of a four-man attacking offense. Moreover, it creates troublesome spaces in the defensive half of the field.

THE FOUR-BACK SYSTEM

The four-back system is a recent development in defensive strategy. It was devised to lessen the effectiveness of the four-man attacking offense. It is a

How may the ball be played if the receiver is the goalkeeper? if he is a fullback? If this is a throw-in, has it been directed to the proper height for the goalkeeper to receive?

difficult defensive system to employ successfully, and it requires highly skilled players who are well versed in all aspects of the game.

The four-back game retains the center halfback as the third back and calls upon one of the wing halfbacks to play as the fourth fullback. It then becomes necessary for one of the forwards to play the halfback position. The alignment of players under these conditions becomes 4-2-4.

The four fullbacks have the primary responsibility of defense. The two outside backs mark the opposing wingmen, and the two center backs stop the down-the-middle attack. The fullbacks, in their roles as defenders, should not cross the halfway line.

The area of play for the halfbacks and forwards remains much the same as in the three-back game. The two halfbacks provide support for the forward line on offense and assist the fullbacks on defense when they are needed.

There are, of course, other defensive systems used by competitive soccer teams. However, most of these systems are too intricate for beginners and require players with considerable ability and knowledge of the game. Therefore, they will not be discussed here. Information concerning these systems can be found in current soccer coaching books and periodicals.

DEVELOPING THE OFFENSE

The two main types of offense are the long-passing and the short-passing attacks. The long-passing attack yields large yardage gains, the element of surprise, and many scoring opportunities, but it reduces control of the ball and cannot be used successfully against a strong wind. The short-passing attack gives better ball control and decreases opportunities for interception, but it requires very accurate passing and good ground conditions. Since each type of attack has its advantages and disadvantages, the type employed should be chosen according to the ability of the players, game situations, and weather conditions.

A and B (team 1) are attempting to move the ball toward their opponent's goal in the direction of the arrow. As Y (team 2) approaches, A passes the ball to B. What mistakes have A and B made?

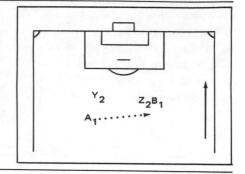

Basic Formations

These formations afford starting points for the attack. The formations should not be viewed as inflexible or unchangeable, since the manner in which the attack finally is carried out depends upon the players and game situations.

The W formation (fig. 5.8), the M formation (fig. 5.9), and the spearhead formation (fig. 5.10))are based on the following principles:

1. Pass the ball to the attack areas or to open spaces near players. For example, in the W formation the inside forwards pass the ball to the attack areas in front of the center or outside forwards.

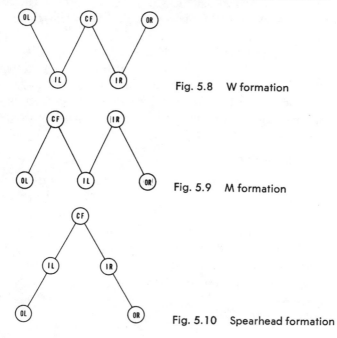

Fig. 5.8   W formation

Fig. 5.9   M formation

Fig. 5.10   Spearhead formation

A_1 (attacking team) shoots the ball at the goal. X_2 (defending team) catches the ball. What should X do now? What should Y_2, Z_2, and A_1 do?

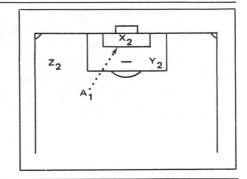

2. Attack in depth, or in waves of players. Players should avoid forming a straight line across the field as they approach the penalty area.

3. Practice interchanging positions in an effort to confuse the defense.

4. Carry the attack on a wide front in order to spread out the defense.

5. Use forward and backward passes to keep your opponent off guard.

6. Switch the play from one side of the field to the other by kicking the ball back and forth across the field.

7. Use elements of surprise and suddenness to outmaneuver your opponent.

8. Notice positions of players so that you can utilize open spaces as the attack unfolds.

9. Set up plays in advance and attempt to carry them out even though teammates may be closely guarded.

Set Plays   Kickoff plays, throw-in plays, corner kicks, and goal kicks are important parts of offensive strategy. Through predetermined and well-practiced sets plays, your team will be able to retain possession of the ball and make progress in advancing toward the opponent's goal.

Kickoff plays are numerous and varied. In order to vary your offense and deceive the opponents, plays should be devised that involve the forwards, the center half, or the halfbacks. An example of a play involving the center half follows:

1. The center forward kicks off to the inside right forward and runs downfield ready to receive a pass.

2. The other forwards also run downfield ready to receive a pass.

3. The inside right forward passes back to the center half, who, in turn, makes a long downfield kick to one of the forwards.

The forwards have decided to use the straight line formation. Is this good strategy? What positions should B and D assume? Have A and E provided the best assistance? Is a "close" formation better than one that is spread out?

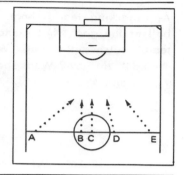

Throw-in plays are important because of the scoring opportunities that can occur as a result of them. The type of throw-in play to be used will be governed by the position of the ball and the tactics of the defense. Other suggestions regarding throw-in plays follow.

1. In general, throw the ball to the feet of all teammates except to the goalkeeper, who should receive the ball chest-high.
2. When in the defensive end of the field, throw the ball away from the goal area, unless throwing directly to the goalkeeper.
3. When near midfield, a throw-in play involving any of a number of players is possible. Don't follow the same procedure all the time.
4. When in the offensive end of the field, a throw-in to any temporarily unmarked player may put the ball into scoring position.

When the goal kick is taken from your own goal, the goalkeeper generally kicks the ball. Duties of the other players then may be as follows:

1. One fullback guards the goal while the goalkeeper kicks.
2. The other fullback marks the opposing center forward.
3. The halfbacks mark the opposing inside forwards.
4. The ball is kicked to either side of midfield, and the forwards set up the attack.

Additional goal kick plays involving other players are possible. In any event, don't follow the same procedure all the time.

The corner kick provides an excellent opportunity for scoring since a goal may be made directly from it. Important points to bear in mind when this situation arises are:

1. Take the corner kick quickly before the defenders can set up a solid defense.

Devise a set play for the kickoff, throw-in, corner kick, or goal kick. Practice the play with your teammates and then try it in a game situation. Did it work? If not, was the play at fault, the situation in which it was used incorrect, or the execution poor?

2. The kicker, usually the outside forward, should vary his kick in both height and spin.
3. Position the forwards to work as a unit when receiving the ball, or move them back to the penalty area line to draw out the defenders.

DEVELOPING THE DEFENSE

The two main types of defense are the zone and man-for-man. In the zone defense each player is responsible for guarding the man with the ball when that man is in his area or zone. This type of defense is recommended for beginning players since it stresses positional play. Its major weakness lies in the fact that it does not provide cover for every man in the attack.

The man-for-man defense requires that each player guard a particular opponent throughout defensive situations no matter where that player is. Although this type of defense provides adequate cover for all attackers, it also requires skilled players. If a player is outmaneuvered by his opponent, it is necessary for one of his teammates to come to his aid.

In order to gain the advantages of each type of defense, a combination zone and man-for-man defense can be employed. The players in the immediate area of the ball mark the attackers in that area. When the ball moves to another area, the players closest to it mark the attackers. Within striking distance of the goal, every player is marked closely.

Basic principles to bear in mind when developing defensive strategy are:

1. Arrange the defense in depth, in waves of players. Avoid forming a straight line of players when nearing your own goal area.
2. Keep your defense in close; the more spread out the defense, the more vulnerable it is.
3. When a teammate tackles the man with the ball, mark the man who is left unguarded. Avoid two-on-one or three-on-two situations.
4. Be ready to provide assistance or to back up play in the area where the ball is located.
5. Retreat slowly when necessary in order to enable your teammates to set up the defense.

6. Pass the ball to the goalkeeper when pressed by the attackers so that he may clear the ball from the goal area.
7. Defensive halfbacks should converge toward the goal as play draws near the goal area.

Soccer, like most games, is largely a matter of using your wits, but before you can outmaneuver your opponent you have to have the skill and knowledge to do so. In addition, the eleven men comprising the soccer team must be able to blend their skills and knowledge so that they perform as an efficient unit rather than as an aimless group of individuals.

INSTRUCTIONAL OBJECTIVES

The purpose of this chapter is to enable each student to—

1. identify the positions and responsibilities of each player on a soccer team,
2. be aware of various defensive and offensive systems used in playing the game,
3. differentiate between the long-passing and short-passing attacks,
4. cite examples of principles that show a basic understanding of offensive and defensive strategies,
5. recognize that set plays are an important part of offensive strategy.

The language and lore of soccer

6

Sports in the United States are the result of an infinite number of influences. A great many of our present sports, including soccer, are not American in origin. Soccer, or a game resembling it, is the oldest team sport in written history. The ancient Greeks played a type of soccer called harpaston. The Romans adopted the game and later introduced it into England. The English version of soccer is considered by many historians to be the origin of the game we know today.

As might be suspected, the game of soccer that became popular with the common people of England had many severe limitations as a sport. Lack of rules, regulations, and general organization led to destruction of property, serious injuries, and loss of life. Consequently, English aristocrats opposed the game, and numerous monarchs outlawed it down through the years. Not until the early seventeenth century was soccer sanctioned by King James I. By 1700 the game was adopted and modified by many English schools, colleges, and clubs.

In the first quarter of the nineteenth century, running with the ball was introduced at Rugby School. This development led to the differentiation now made between soccer and football. By the 1830s soccer was played in American colleges under varied rules. During the 1860s the London Football Association was formed in England. This association determined the rules and regulations which governed the game of soccer.

In America, Rutgers and Princeton Universities played the first intercollegiate soccer game in 1869. A continued lack of uniformity in rules finally led to the formation of the Intercollegiate Association Football

League during the early 1900s. This organization functioned until 1925. Soccer became a part of the Olympic Games in 1900 and has remained quite popular over the years.

The United States Football Association, which was founded in 1913, was accepted in affiliation with the Federation Internationale de Football Association in 1914. In 1945 the name was changed to the United States Soccer Football Association (USSFA). The Intercollegiate Soccer Football Association of America became an active member of the USSFA in 1926.

The USSFA organized tournament play for the National (Open) Challenge Cup in 1913. Originally this tournament was for amateur play only, but today it is open to all professional and amateur teams in the United States. It is soccer's most coveted award in this country. In 1922 the need for a separate award for amateur teams became evident. As a result, the USSFA established the National Amateur Challenge Cup, which is a tournament for amateur teams only.

The Jules Rimet trophy, or World Cup, which was established in 1930, is the emblem of world supremacy in soccer. To the soccer world, the World Cup tournament is like the Olympic Games; and it occurs every four years midway between the Olympic years. It is commonly called the World Series of sport since soccer teams from most of the countries in the world compete in the tournament.

Past winners of the World Cup include Uruguay, Italy, West Germany, Brazil, and England. Prior to 1970, Uruguay, Italy, and Brazil had won the world championship twice. According to the rules, the team that wins the cup three times gains permanent possession of it, although world championship matches will continue to be played. In the 1970 World Cup tournament all three teams advanced to the semifinals with Brazil defeating Italy for the world soccer title and permanent possession of the Jules Rimet Cup. The 1974 World Cup Championship, which was held in Munich, was of interest to millions of soccer fans throughout the world. It has been estimated that a worldwide television audience of one billion watched West Germany defeat Holland by a score of 2 to 1.

Within recent years there has been greater interest in soccer in the United States. The International Soccer League (ISL), which was formed in 1960, brought international championship teams to play games in many of the larger cities of the United States. It has been estimated that in its first five years of operation the ISL had a total attendance of over one million people. This league ceased to function after 1965. Past exhibition games between outstanding international teams have drawn record-breaking crowds ranging from twenty-eight thousand to over forty thousand fans for a single game.

In 1967 the organization of two professional soccer leagues in the United States further increased interest and enthusiasm for the game. The United Soccer Association, which was recognized by the USSFA and FIFA, organized a twelve-team league. The National Professional Soccer League, which was not recognized by the USSFA or the FIFA, organized a ten-team league. Both of these leagues played scheduled league games during 1967. However, dwindling attendance (average attendance was five thousand per game) caused financial problems. The two leagues merged to become the North American Soccer League (NASL) in 1968, and the league consisted of five professional teams in 1969. Within the last few years soccer interest in the United States has been increasing. The NASL disclosed that figures for the 1974 opening games revealed a vast improvement in attendance. By 1975 there were twenty teams in the league. The NASL is also planning a United States team for the 1978 World Cup Competition.

SOCCER TERMS

Charging.   A method of unbalancing your opponent when he has possession or is attempting to gain possession of the ball.

Clearing.   A throw or kick by the goalkeeper after he has stopped a ball in the vicinity of the goal area.

Corner Kick.   A kick made by the attacking team from a corner arc. A corner kick is awarded when the ball is last touched by a defensive player and passes over the goal line without resulting in a goal.

Cross.   A ball kicked from one side of the field to the other side.

Dangerous Play.   Play that is likely to cause injury. Raising the foot shoulder-high, attempting to head a ball below waist level, or executing a double kick within six feet of a player, for example, constitute dangerous play.

Direct Free Kick.   A free kick from which a goal can be scored directly. It is awarded for personal fouls and major infractions of the rules.

Dribbling.   A method of advancing the ball with the feet by a series of short taps.

Drop Ball.   A ball held by the referee and allowed to fall directly to the ground between two opponents. The ball is in play when it touches the ground. A goal may be scored directly from a drop ball.

Feint Movements.   Movements of the body, especially the knees and feet, made for the purpose of deceiving your opponent as to your real intention.

Goal.   A one-point score occuring when the ball passes wholly over the goal line, between the goalposts, and under the crossbar.

Goal Kick.   An indirect free kick made by any defending player from the goal box. A goal kick is awarded when the ball is last touched by an offensive player and passes over the goal line without resulting in a goal.

Goalkeeper.   A player designated to guard the goal. The "goalie" may run with the ball and touch it with his hands under specified conditions; these are special privileges that no other player enjoys.

Handling.   The act of carrying, striking, or propelling the ball with the hand or arm.

Heading.   A method of passing, scoring, or bringing the ball under control by allowing it to come in contact with the forehead.

Immunity.   The goalkeeper may not be charged in the penalty area. While he has possession of the ball, an opponent may not interfere in any manner.

Indirect Free Kick.   A free kick from which a goal cannot be scored until the ball is touched by another player. It is awarded for technical and minor infractions of the rules.

Instep.   The top portion of the foot covered by the shoelace.

Instep Kick.   A long kick performed by making contact with the ball at the instep or shoelace.

Kickoff.   A place kick from the center spot within the center circle that puts the ball into play at the beginning of each quarter and after each score. The kickoff rule specifies conditions of play.

Loft or Lob.   A high, soft kick.

Marking.   Guarding or covering the player with the ball when he moves into your area of play.

Obstruction.   A method of blocking the path an opponent wishes to take when you are not playing the ball.

Penalty Box.   That area directly in front of the mouth of the goal (eighteen by forty-five yards). The goalkeeper may use his hands in this area only.

Penalty Kick.   A direct free kick from a spot (penalty mark) twelve yards from the goal line. It is awarded to the offended team for fouls committed by the defensive team in its own penalty area.

Save.   A shot at the goal that is stopped by the goalkeeper.

Tackling.   A method of gaining possession of the ball by use of the feet. Unnecessary roughness and use of the hands are not permitted.

Throw-In.   A two-handed, over-the-head throw that puts the ball into play after it has gone out of play over a touchline.

Touchline.   The boundary lines on each side of the field.

Unintentional Handling.   The ball touches the hands or arms of a player.

No penalty is awarded even if the offending team gains an advantage.
Volleying.   Kicking the ball while it is in the air.

INSTRUCTIONAL OBJECTIVES

The purpose of this chapter is to enable each student to—

1. become familiar with the historical development and present status of soccer as a national and international sport,
2. conclude that soccer is a worldwide sport that is gaining enthusiastic support in the United States,
3. define the meanings of terms that are peculiar to soccer.

Rules of the Game

7

A summary of the most important rules of soccer is presented in the following pages. Those students who desire a more detailed analysis of the rules should refer to *The Official NCAA Soccer Guide*.[1]

RULE FOUR

The game is started from the center spot within the center circle by means of a *place* kick into the opponent's half of the field of play. The following stipulations govern the kickoff:

1. Before the ball is kicked, every player must be in his own half of the field.
2. Players of the opposing team must be outside the center circle (ten yards away) until the ball travels *forward* at least the distance of its circumference, i.e., twenty-seven inches.
3. A goal cannot be scored directly from a kickoff.
4. The player who kicks the ball cannot play it a second time until it has been played or touched by another player.
5. The ball can be kicked in any direction by any player after a proper kickoff.

1. Adapted from the NCAA Publishing Service, *The Official National Collegiate Athletic Association Soccer Guide* (Shawnee Mission, Kansas: NCAA Publishing Service, 1974).

Penalty for Improper Kickoff

1. The kickoff is retaken for an infringement of stipulations 1, 2, or 3.
2. An indirect free kick is awarded to the opposing team for an infringement of stipulation 4.

After a goal is scored, the ball is kicked off by the team against which the goal was scored. At the start of the second half, teams change ends of the field, and the team that kicked off at the start of the previous period receives the kickoff.

The ball is put into play by means of a drop ball for any other temporary suspension of play, except in the case of a free kick or a throw-in. The drop occurs at the point where the ball was when play was suspended, and players cannot touch the ball until it touches the ground. If play is suspended when the ball is in the penalty area, the ball is dropped at the nearest point outside the penalty area.

The markings on the soccer field are considered in play. The ball is therefore in play until it completely crosses the goal or touchlines either in the air or on the ground. In addition, the ball is in play if it returns to the field of play after striking a goalpost, crossbar, or corner flag. It is also in play if it touches either referee in the field of play.

In all cases, it is the position of the ball that is important. For example, a ball in the air that passes out of play and returns to the field of play should be given out of play, or as long as the ball remains inside the field of play, a player outside the playing area may play the ball.

In order to score a goal, the ball must completely cross the goal line, between the goalposts, and under the crossbar. The attacking team cannot score a goal by using the hands or arms.

RULE FIVE

The *offside* rule prevents a player from interfering with an opponent or with the play. It also prevents a player from remaining close to the goal area where a goal could be scored from short range. If a player is nearer his opponent's goal line than the ball when the ball is played, he is offside unless:

1. He is in his own half of the field of play.
2. There are two of his opponents *nearer* to their goal line than he.
3. The ball last touched an opponent or was last played by him.
4. He receives the ball directly from a goal kick, corner kick, throw-in, or drop by the referee.

A steps out-of-bounds to kick the ball, which is in bounds, to B. Should the ball be called in play or out of play?

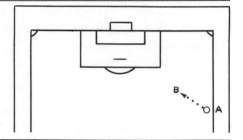

Penalty for Infraction of Offside Rule

1. An indirect free kick is taken by a player of the opposing team.
2. An offside player is not penalized unless he is interfering with play or seeking to gain an advantage.

RULE SIX

Penalties are imposed upon players who commit *intentional* fouls or are involved in misconduct such as:

1. Kicking, striking, or jumping at an opponent.
2. Tripping or stooping in front of an opponent.
3. Handling the ball (other than the goalkeeper when he is in his own penalty area).
4. Holding, pushing, obstructing with the hand or arm, or using the knee against an opponent.
5. Charging an opponent in a violent or dangerous manner.
6. Charging the goalkeeper in the penalty area.
7. Kicking the ball when it is in the possession of the goalkeeper.
8. Obstructing an opponent, i.e., running between an opponent and the ball or using the body as an obstacle to block the path of an opponent.

RULE SEVEN

Free kicks are classified as direct, from which a goal can be scored directly, and indirect, from which a goal cannot be scored until the ball has been touched by another player. Direct free kicks are awarded for major infractions of the rules and for personal misconduct. (Direct kicks awarded to the offensive team in the penalty area are penalty kicks; a free kick awarded to the defensive team in the penalty area must be kicked out of the penalty area.) Offenses for which a direct free kick is given include:

A₁ (attacking team) shoots the ball at the goal. X₂ (defending team) catches the ball and plays it so that B₁ gains possession. B₁ shoots and scores a goal. Is A₁ or B₁ offside?

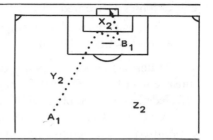

1. Offenses committed with the hands or arms (handling the ball, holding, using hands or arms on an opponent in order to reach the ball, pushing, and striking).
2. Offenses committed with the feet and legs (kicking, tripping, use of the knee, and jumping at an opponent).
3. Offenses concerned with charging violently or dangerously (failure of both players to be in an upright position, to be within playing distance of the ball, to have at least one foot on the ground, or to hold the arms close to the body).
4. Offenses involving the goalkeeper (handling by the goalkeeper outside the penalty area, handling by a new goalkeeper who has failed to properly notify the referee, charging the goalkeeper while he is in the penalty area, and intentionally throwing or striking an opponent with the ball by the goalkeeper).

Indirect free kicks are awarded for minor infractions of the rules and for technical violations. Offenses for which an indirect free kick is given include:

1. Offenses concerned with a player kicking the ball a second time before it is played by another player (kickoffs, throw-in, free kick, corner kick, and goal kick if the ball has passed outside the penalty area).
2. Offenses committed during the penalty kick (ball not kicked forward).
3. Offenses involving the goalkeeper (carrying the ball by the goalkeeper more than four steps without bouncing it, and delaying the game by not getting rid of the ball).
4. Offenses involving persons on the sidelines (substitution made at improper time, substitute failing to report to the referee, illegal coaching from sidelines after a warning).
5. Offenses concerned with unsportsmanlike conduct (arguing with the referee, ungentlemanly conduct, dangerous play, and failure to leave the field of play after ordered to do so).

6. Offenses concerned with offside.

7. Offenses concerned with improper charging, interfering with goalkeeper, obstruction other than holding.

When a free kick is being taken, all members of the opposing team must remain ten yards away from the ball until it is in play, i.e., until it has traveled the distance of its circumference.

A *penalty kick* is awarded to the offended team for *deliberate* fouls committed by the defensive team in its own penalty area. Infringements of the rules must be those that are penalized by a direct free kick. The kick is taken from the penalty mark. The following stipulations govern the penalty kick:

1. Only the player taking the kick and the opposing goalkeeper may play the ball.

2. All other players must be outside the penalty area, at least ten yards from the penalty mark but within the field of play.

3. Without moving his feet, the goalkeeper must stand on the goal line until the ball is kicked.

4. The player must kick the ball forward, and he cannot play the ball a second time until it has been touched by another player.

Penalty for Improper Penalty Kick

1. The kick is retaken for an infringement of the foregoing stipulations by the defending team if a goal has not resulted.

2. The kick is retaken for an infringement by any member of the attacking team other than the player kicking the ball if a goal is scored.

3. An indirect free kick is awarded to the opposing team for an infringement by the player kicking the ball.

A *throw-in* from the touchline is awarded when the ball passes completely over a touchline either on the ground or in the air. The ball is thrown in from the spot where it crossed the touchline. The following stipulations govern the throw-in:

1. The throw-in is taken by a player of the team opposite to that of the player who last touched the ball.

2. The thrower must face the field of play and must have part of each foot either on the touchline or on the ground outside the touchline at the moment he delivers the ball.

3. The thrower must use both hands equally and must deliver the ball from behind and over his head.

A (attacking team) shoots for a goal. Y (defending team) intentionally strikes the ball with his hand. Has a foul occurred? If so, under what conditions is the ball put into play?

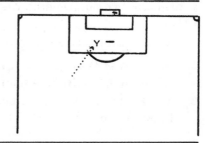

4. The ball may be thrown in any direction.
5. The thrower may not play the ball a second time until it has been touched by another player.
6. A goal cannot be scored directly from a throw-in.

Penalty for improper throw-in:

1. The throw-in is taken by a player of the opposing team for an infringement of stipulations 2 or 3.
2. An indirect free kick is awarded to the opposing team for an infringement of stipulation 5.

A *goal kick* is awarded when the ball is last touched by an offensive player and passes over the goal line without resulting in a goal. The kick is made by a defender from a point within that half of the goal area nearest to where the ball crossed the line. The following stipulations govern the goal kick:

1. The ball must be kicked from the ground in any direction beyond the penalty area.
2. The kicker cannot play the ball a second time until it has been touched by another player.
3. A goal cannot be scored directly from a goal kick since it is an indirect free kick.

Penalty for Improper Goal Kick

1. The kick is retaken if the ball is not kicked beyond the penalty area.
2. An indirect free kick is awarded to the opposing team for an infringement by the player who is kicking.

A *corner kick* is awarded when the ball is last touched by a defensive player and passes over the goal line without resulting in a goal. The kick is made by a member of the attacking team from within the quarter-circle at the nearest corner flag post. The following stipulations govern the corner kick:

1. A goal may be scored directly from such a kick.
2. Members of the opposing team must remain ten yards away from the ball until it travels the distance of its circumference.
3. The kicker cannot play the ball a second time until it has been touched by another player.

Penalty for Improper Corner Kick

1. The kick is retaken for an infringement of stipulation 2.
2. An indirect free kick is awarded to the opposing team for an infringement of stipulation 3.

INSTRUCTIONAL OBJECTIVES

The purpose of this chapter is to enable each student to—

1. examine the most important rules of soccer,
2. synthesize information pertaining to each of the rules of the game,
3. accurately interpret game rules in order to improve skill in and enjoyment of the game.

Unwritten rules

8

Courtesy and sportsmanship are as much a part of sports activities as are the skills and rules of the game. No one enjoys playing a game with a person who is a "hothead" or a "complainer," and no doubt those individuals who cannot control their emotions do not really enjoy the game. This certainly does not mean that you must give up aggressive play or the will to win; however, it does mean that each player has the responsibility of developing emotional control. Learning to accept situations as they occur and developing respect for your teammates, your opponents, and the officials are major steps in this direction. Remember that courtesy and sportsmanship cannot be imposed on players by means of rules. These concepts emerge only as individual players gain understanding of and respect for the spirit of rules. The following list of game courtesies should help you develop better sportsmanship and increase your enjoyment of soccer.

1. Always play your best and play to win, but play for fun.
2. When you are aware that you have committed an infringement of the rules, notify the official by raising your hand over your head. For example, if you touched the ball last before it went out-of-bounds, or if you touched the ball with your hand or arm, raise your hand.
3. Leave your temper and inappropriate language in the locker room. Derogatory remarks will not improve your game.
4. Keep the game moving. Move the required distance from the ball for free kicks as quickly as possible. Be ready to start play immediately upon the referee's signal.

5. Don't criticize the play of others, and don't blame others for your own poor playing.
6. Be humble in victory and gracious in defeat.
7. Congratulate your opponent, and extend thanks to the officials after the game, whether you win or lose.

INSTRUCTIONAL OBJECTIVES

The purpose of this chapter is to enable each student to—

1. examine, interpret, and apply unwritten rules in relation to game situations.

Facts for enthusiasts

9

FACTS ABOUT EQUIPMENT

Unless you become a member of an organized soccer team or club, you will find that very little personal equipment is needed to enjoy the game. For most school or recreational purposes, all that actually is needed is a soccer ball and wearing apparel appropriate to vigorous activity. Even then, the soccer ball does not have to meet official specifications.

As members of a team or club, players wear jerseys, shorts, a special soccer shoe, shin guards, and long stockings. The soccer shoe is the most important part of the player's equipment. A regulation shoe is high-laced and cleated with aluminum, leather, rubber, nylon, or steel tipped plastic to prevent slipping. The shoe must conform to specifications related to the width and length of cleats.

The official soccer ball must meet several specifications concerned with inflation, circumference, and weight. The leather covered soccer ball must be 27 to 28 inches in circumference and 14 to 16 ounces in weight at the start of the game. It cannot exceed 16.75 ounces even when wet and used. The inflation pressure of the ball is not stated in pounds but rather is indicated by stating the number of inches (100) from which it must be dropped to a smooth cement surface and the number of inches (60 to 65) to which it must rebound.

When selecting equipment such as shoes or a ball, you should keep several points in mind. The shoes should be of a good grade of leather and should fit comfortably. Proper drying of shoes after use and proper storage of shoes when not in use are important aspects of their care.

Whether you select a rubber-covered ball or a leather-covered ball is a matter of personal preference. The rubber-covered ball is an all-purpose ball and requires little care. The leather-covered ball should be cleaned periodically with saddle soap or a similar cleaner. If the ball becomes wet, it should be placed in a warm room to dry. Both the rubber- and leather-covered balls should be partially deflated and stored in a dry place when not in use.

FACTS ABOUT CURRENT PLAY

The Intercollegiate Soccer Football Association and the National Collegiate Athletic Association have sponsored the NCAA tournament since 1959. The St. Louis University Billikens have dominated intercollegiate soccer since its inception. A victory in the 1973 championship finals gave the Billikens their tenth National Collegiate Championship in fifteen years. Other teams that have won the NCAA tournament include the United States Naval Academy, the University of San Francisco, Michigan State University, the University of Maryland, and Howard University.

There are many international "heroes" or outstanding players of the game. Edson Arantes Do Nascimento, or as he is known in the soccer world, Pelé, is probably the world's finest soccer player. His accomplishment of scoring the one thousandth goal of his professional career has made him the top goal scorer in professional and modern soccer. In 1974, Pelé announced his retirement from soccer. The New York Cosmos, however, were able to lure the thirty-four-year-old star back to the game. He made his debut for the Cosmos in June, 1975.

INSTRUCTIONAL OBJECTIVES

The purpose of this chapter is to enable each student to—

1. recognize that there are many soccer enthusiasts throughout the world,
2. conclude that very little personal soccer equipment is needed to play the game,
3. cite examples to show the importance of selection and care of equipment.

Playing the game

10

Learning to play soccer represents a distinct challenge to most Americans since most of our sports place emphasis upon eye-hand coordination. Once that basic skills and knowledges of the unique game of soccer are learned, however, interest and enthusiasm in it spread rapidly. Undoubtedly soccer is played in many places in your community. It is generally played in the public schools in physical education classes, in intramural programs, and in interscholastic programs. It is also played in recreation programs and camps.

If there is a college or university in or near your community, the chances are good that you can see soccer played in classes, intramurally, and interscholastically. You can also see soccer games in cities that have amateur and professional soccer teams. In addition, you can watch professional and international soccer games on television.

You can read about soccer in the sports pages of many newspapers. *Soccer America* and *Soccer World* are weekly publications devoted to soccer. Popular magazines such as *Time, Newsweek, Reader's Digest, Sports Illustrated* and other sports magazines occasionally publish articles about soccer.

If you are interested in soccer from the teaching or coaching point of view, the *Athletic Journal* and the *Scholastic Coach* publish numerous articles. Also available are a monthly publication by the United States Soccer Football Association entitled *Soccer News* and a quarterly publication by the National Soccer Coaches of America entitled *Soccer Journal.*

Soccer tournaments are generally of either the single elimination or the round-robin type. In most schools and colleges, the round-robin type of tournament is popular. This type of tournament places the teams in leagues; each team in the league plays every other team in that league. At the end of league play, the winner is determined on the basis of percentage points and, in some cases, a single elimination tournament among the league leaders to determine the championship.

INSTRUCTIONAL OBJECTIVES

The purpose of this chapter is to enable each student to—

1. locate various places in his community where soccer is played,
2. identify newspapers and magazines that publish articles about soccer.

References and resources

ALLISON, MALCOLM. *Soccer for Thinkers.* London: Pelham Books, 1971.

DE BOER, KLASS. "Corner Kick Alternatives." *Athletic Journal* 53 (April 1973): 20.

DI CLEMENTE, FRANK F. *Soccer Illustrated.* New York: The Ronald Press, 1968.

GAMMON, C. "Where a Cup Is Bigger Than a Stein." *Sports Illustrated* 13 May 1974, p. 80.

HERRMANN, KARL T. "Developing Individual Ball Control Skills in Soccer." *Athletic Journal* 50 (September 1969):103.

———. "Make Your Soccer Drills Functional." *Athletic Journal* 52 (April 1972):54.

———. "All-Out Pressure Defense in Soccer." *Athletic Journal* 53 (June 1973): 6.

KEETON, GEORGE W. *The Football Revolution.* Newton Abbot: David and Charles Publishers, 1972.

LEVIN, DAN. "The Penalty for Success." *Sports Illustrated* 2 September 1974, p. 14.

MAULE, TEX. "Pelé and Pals Retire the Cup." *Sports Illustrated* 29 June 1970, p. 24.

———. "Soccer Is a Frenzy." *Sports Illustrated* 22 June 1970, p. 12.

———. "They Knew a Way to San Jose." *Sports Illustrated* 5 August 1974, p. 14.

———. "They're All Right, Jack." *Sports Illustrated* 25 February 1974, p. 56.

MENENDEZ, JULIE, and BOXER, MATT. *Soccer.* New York: The Ronald Press, 1968.

MENKE, FRANK G. *The Encyclopedia of Sports.* South Brunswick, N.J.: A. S. Barnes and Company, 1969.

NCAA Publishing Service. *The Official National Collegiate Athletic Association Soccer Guide.* Shawnee Mission, Kansas: NCAA Publishing Service, 1974.

"Passion Called Soccer." *Newsweek* 8 July 1974, p. 63.

REEVES, J. A. "Simpler the Better for Soccer Drills." *Athletic Journal* 52 (March 1972):46.

ROTE, K. "Learning The Game By Rote." *"Sports Illustrated* 6 August 1973, p. 30.

SCHMID, IRVIN R. et al. *Skills and Strategies of Successful Soccer.* Englewood Cliffs, N.J.: Prentice-Hall, 1968.

SCHULTS, FREDERICK D. "Pelé Style." *Athletic Journal* 51 (June 1971):20.

SIMON, J. MALCOM, and DEVITO, LOUIS. "Soccer's 4-2-4 System." *Athletic Journal* 46 (September 1965):54.

VOGELSINGER, HUBERT. *Winning Soccer Skills and Techniques.* New York: Parker Publishing Company, 1970.

———. *The Challenge of Soccer.* Boston: Allyn and Bacon, 1973.

WADE, ALLEN. *Soccer: Guide to Training and Coaching.* New York: Funk and Wagnalls, 1967.

YASINAC, JOHN. "Pressure Drills for the Soccer Goalkeeper." *Athletic Journal* 52 (September 1971):46.

LIST OF RESOURCES

The New York Times Index.

Soccer America, P.O. Box 23704, Oakland, Calif. 94623. (Published weekly.) Printed by B & B Printing, Albany. Business Address: 1519 Shattuck Avenue, Berkeley, Calif. 94709.

Soccer Journal, National Soccer Coaches Association of America, 668 La Vista Creek, Walnut Creek, California 94598. (Published quarterly.)

Soccer News, Soccer Associates, Inc., Box 634, New Rochelle, New York 10802. (Published monthly.)

Soccer World, World Publications, Box 366, Mountain View, California 94040. (Published weekly.)

AUDIO-VISUAL MATERIALS

Films

Fundamentals of Soccer. Analyzes basic and advanced skills and shows their uses in game situations (13 minutes; b & w). All American Productions and Publishers, P.O. Box 91, Greeley, Colorado 80632.

Pass Dribble Shoot. Emphasizes basic skills, practice formations, and game situations (11 minutes; color). Soccer U.S.A., P. O. Box 4152, Pasadena, California 91106.

Soccer: Let's Play. An excellent presentation of beginning soccer skills (10 minutes; color). University of Utah, Education Media Center, Milton Bennion Hall 207, Salt Lake City, Utah 84110.

Soccer's Here. Shows the pageantry of international soccer and explains the game as it takes place on the field (21 minutes; color). Soccer U.S.A., P.O. Box 4152, Pasadena, California 91106.

Teams in Action. Explains the rules of the game, soccer skills, game strategies, and the long and short pass styles of play (17 minutes; color). Soccer U.S.A., P.O. Box 4152, Pasadena, California 91106.

Loop Films

Soccer. Individual loop films stressing basic and advanced skills, team play, and game strategies. Encyclopaedia Britannica Educational Corporation, 425 North Michigan Avenue, Chicago, Illinois 60611.

Soccer. Individual loop films stressing basic and advanced skills, team play, and game strategies. NCAA Films, P.O. Box 2726, Wichita, Kansas 67201.

Appendix: Questions and answers

MULTIPLE CHOICE

1. The game of soccer is played in more than_____nations.
   a. 80   b. 100   c. 110   D. 130   (p. 3)

2. Within recent years the popularity of soccer in the United States has
   A. increased tremendously   c. decreased slowly
   b. remained the same   d. decreased rapidly   (p. 3)

3. A volley kick is executed when the ball is
   a. rolling on the ground
   b. stationary on the ground
   c. at least as high as the head
   D. in the air, either before or after it bounces   (p. 6)

4. The instep kick is
   a. mainly used for short passes
   B. used when both power and accuracy are needed
   c. less effective when the ball is bouncing
   d. is not a skill pertaining to soccer   (p. 4)

5. The inside of the foot kicks are good for short passes, but they
   A. are not too deceptive
   b. lead to lack of ball control
   c. encourage bunching up the players
   d. lead to tripping and stumbling over the ball   (p. 6)

6. Which of the following statements related to kicking is incorrect?
   a. Keep your eyes on the ball at all times.
   b. Your body should be relaxed, especially the kicking leg.
   C. Practice kicking on a fast moving ball.
   d. Know the direction and distance you want the ball to travel.   (p. 4)

7. When performing the flick or jab, you should try to_____the ball with the outside of the foot.
   a. kick   B. jab   c. loft   d. deflect   (p. 7)

8. Which of the following statements concerning dribbling is correct?
   a. Kick rather than push or tap the ball.
   b. Work for speed rather than ball control.
   C. Keep the ball near the feet throughout the dribble.
   d. Swerving, feigning, and change of pace make dribbling much less effective.

   (p.12)

9. The process of bringing the ball under your control is called
   a. charging   b. dribbling   c. passing   D. trapping   (p. 7)

10. When executing the stomach or chest trap, you should
    A. jump off both feet and allow your body to "give"
    b. cover the abdomen or chest with your arms
    c. jump toward the ball with the body rigid
    d. flex one knee, raising the foot off the ground three to four inches   (p. 10)

11. Which of the following statements concerning passing is incorrect?
    a. The passer must be sure he can pass the ball without its being intercepted.
    B. Accuracy is of little importance if the ball is kicked skillfully.
    c. The passer should pass only to an unmarked teammate.
    d. The passer must be able to kick the ball with enough skill so that the
       receiver can gain control of it.   (p. 11)

12. A good method of gaining control of a ball in low flight is the
    a. half-volley kick
    b. chest trap
    c. stomach trap
    D. inside of the thigh trap   (p. 10)

13. The outside of the foot dribble
    A. increases the speed of the dribbler
    b. is easy to execute
    c. increases ball control
    d. reduces the speed of the dribbler   (p. 19)

14. A tackle is considered successful if you
    a. physically drag your opponent to the ground
    b. knock your opponent off balance
    C. take the ball from your opponent by use of the feet
    d. tag your opponent with one hand between the shoulders and knees   (p. 16)

15. Which of the following is essential to safety when heading the ball?
    a. Push off or climb up your opponent whenever possible.
    B. Never head a ball lower than waist height.
    c. Charge your opponent while he is in the air heading the ball.
    d. Be the first to head the ball, regardless of its height, if you expect to gain
       control of it.   (p. 15)

16. The pivot instep kick is used for _____ balls.
    a. bouncing   b. high fly   c. low fly   D. ground   (p. 18)

17. Positional play for fullbacks requires that these players
    A. remain in their own half of the field to help protect the goal area
    b. remain directly opposite each other at all times
    c. assist the forwards in scoring attempts
    d. avoid entering the goal area since they cannot use their hands   (p. 37)

18. When a fullback covers the goal for the goalie, he
    a. has the same privileges as the goalie
    b. must remain in the goal box in order to handle the ball

C. cannot touch the ball with his hands
d. may catch the ball, but he cannot run with it   (p. 38)

19. Because of his position of play, the_____has the best opportunity for directing the team's defense.
    a. right fullback   c. left fullback
    B. goalie   d. center halfback   (p. 37)

20. Positional play for the right and left halfbacks requires that these players
    a. remain directly opposite each other at all times
    B. assist the forwards in scoring attempts
    c. remain in their own half of the field to help protect the goal area
    d. follow up attempted goal shots in an effort to get a second try for a goal (p. 39)

21. The goalkeeper has the privilege of using his hands to play the ball
    a. anywhere in the field of play
    b. anywhere outside the penalty area
    C. within the penalty area only
    d. only when the fullbacks are outside the penalty area   (p. 36)

22. Good goaltending implies that the goalkeeper should
    a. remain on the goal line to be sure that the ball does not cross it
    b. leave the goal unguarded, if necessary, to assist the fullbacks
    c. remain within the goal box at all times
    D. slowly move out in front of the goal box to pick up a potential scorer   (p. 36)

23. This player, by playing a waiting game, can distract the opponent and be fresh as the attack gets underway.
    A. center forward   c. outside right
    b. inside right   d. center halfback   (p. 40)

24. One of the main types of offense in soccer is the
    a. man-for-man passing game   c. set offense
    B. long passing game   d. dribbling offense   (p. 43)

25. The_____is in the best position to direct the attack.
    a. outside right   c. left halfback
    b. center forward   D. center halfback   (p. 39)

26. Because of their position of play, the_____can use dribbling to a distinct advantage.
    a. inside forwards   C. outside forwards
    b. halfbacks   d. fullbacks   (p. 41)

27. The outside forwards
    A. must be able to stay with or ahead of the ball at all times
    b. play a waiting game so they are fresh when the attack gets underway
    c. act in the capacity of playmakers
    d. are usually responsible for throw-ins   (p. 40)

28. Defensively, the inside forward must mark the opposing
    a. fullback   c. center forward
    b. outside forward   D. halfback   (p. 40)

29. In the three-back system, one of the major responsibilities of the third back is
    a. directing the attack   c. setting up plays
    b. providing a decoy   D. assisting on defense   (p. 42)

30. Regardless of the type of offensive formations used, the offense should never
    a. carry the attack on a wide front so as to spread out the defense
    b. switch the play from one side of the field to the other by crossing the ball

C. attack in a straight line across the field as the penalty area is approached
d. use backward passes in an effort to keep the defense off guard (p. 45)

31. Which of the following statements concerning defensive strategy is most correct?
    a. Avoid passing the ball to the goalkeeper when pressed by the attackers.
    B. The more spread out the defense, the more vulnerable it is.
    c. Avoid arranging the defense in depth or waves.
    d. When a retreat is necessary, retreat quickly in order to set up your defense.
    (p. 47)

32. The man-for-man defense requires that each player marks
    A. a particular opponent throughout defensive situations
    b. the man with the ball when he is in his area
    c. the man with the ball when he is in his half of the field
    d. the man with the ball when he is in the opponent's half of the field (p. 47)

33. Early English aristocrats disliked the game of soccer because
    a. their teams were easily defeated by the teams of the common people
    b. it required considerable expensive equipment which the common people could not afford
    C. inadequate rules and poor organization led to loss of life and destruction of property
    d. it interfered with their leisure-time sports such as hunting and gambling
    (p. 49)

34. The emblem of world supremacy in soccer is the
    a. Davis Cup   c. Stanley Cup
    B. World Cup   d. National Open Challenge Cup   (p. 50)

35. The corner kick provides an excellent opportunity for scoring since
    a. the ball must be kicked toward the mouth of the goal
    b. this kick is the same as an indirect free kick
    c. the ball is put into play by the defending team
    D. a goal may be scored directly from it   (p. 60)

36. Many historians consider the _____version of soccer to be the origin of the game we play today.
    A. English   b. Roman   c. Greek   d. Persian   (p. 49)

37. Which of the following stipulations governing the kickoff is incorrect?
    a. Before the ball is kicked, every player must be in his own half of the field.
    b. Players of the opposing team must be outside the center circle until the ball is kicked.
    C. The player who kicks the ball may dribble it if he notifies the official of his intention.
    d. After a proper kickoff, the ball can be kicked in any direction by any player.
    (p. 54)

38. The change in the game of soccer that distinguished it from football was
    a. aerial passing   c. the number of players on the team
    b. the shape of the ball   D. running with the ball   (p. 49)

39. The governing body of American soccer today is the
    A. United States Soccer Football Association
    b. Intercollegiate Soccer Football Association
    c. United States High School Soccer Association
    d. Federation Internationale de Football Association   (p. 50)

40. All opposing team members must remain_____yards from the ball for free kicks.
    a. five   B. ten   c. fifteen   d. twenty   (p. 58)

41. The official should call the ball out of play when it
    a. touches any out-of-bounds line
    b. strikes a goalpost, crossbar, or corner flag
    c. is in bounds and is kicked by a player who is out-of-bounds
    D. is in the air and passes out of play, but returns to the field of play   (p. 55)

42. On the kickoff, the ball is dribbled by the player who kicks the ball. In this instance
    a. there is no violation of the kickoff rule
    b. the kick is retaken by the offending team
    C. an indirect free kick is awarded to the opposing team
    d. a direct free kick is awarded to the opposing team   (p. 55)

43. When the defensive team deliberately commits a foul in its own penalty area, the offended team is awarded a
    a. goal kick   c. corner kick
    B. penalty kick   d. direct free kick   (p. 58)

44. Which of the following is not an offense for which a direct free kick is given?
    a. handling the ball   c. charging violently
    b. jumping at an opponent   D. ungentlemanly conduct   (p. 57)

45. A kick from which a goal cannot be scored directly is classified as
    A. an indirect free kick   c. a direct free kick
    b. a corner kick   d. a penalty kick   (p. 56)

46. The most important piece of equipment for a soccer player is the
    a. shinguard   c. stocking
    B. shoe   d. headgear   (p. 63)

47. The penalty for jumping into the air while executing a throw-in is
    a. an indirect free kick
    b. a direct free kick
    C. a throw-in awarded to the opposing team
    d. a severe warning by the official   (p. 59)

48. A kick taken from within the quarter-circle at a corner flag post is called a
    a. goal kick   c. free kick
    b. penalty kick   D. corner kick   (p. 59)

49. Courtesy and sportsmanship in soccer imply that you
    A. develop emotional control
    b. give up aggressive play
    c. criticize your opponent and the officials only when they can't hear you
    d. give up the will to win   (p. 61)

50. Internationally_____ is considered to be the finest soccer player.
    a. Eusebio   b. Torres   C. Pelé   d. Sandro   (p. 64)

51. The ability of the whole body, or part of it, to apply force defines
    A. strength   b. tonus   c. endurance   d. fatigue   (p. 30)

52. The alignment of players when using the four-back system is
    a. 4-3-4   b. 4-1-6   C. 4-2-4   d. 4-3-3   (p. 43)

TRUE OR FALSE

t F   53. The fact that soccer is often called the "universal" game is misleading since only a relatively few countries play the game.   (p. 3)

T f   54. The game of soccer, unlike most games played in the United States, is played primarily with the feet.   (p. 1)

t F   55. To perform the push pass, place the inside of the foot slightly under the ball and lift as you kick.   (p. 7)

t F   56. To execute the instep kick correctly, the toe of the shoe should contact the ball slightly below its midpoint.   (p. 5)

T f   57. The sole of the foot trap can be used to trap a rolling or bouncing ball.   (p. 8)

T f   58. When passing the ball, you should look at the ball while in the act of kicking.   (p. 12)

t F   59. A simple rule to follow is dribble the ball whenever possible rather than pass.   (p. 12)

T f   60. The throw-in is important because it is a method of restarting play and initiating offensive play.   (p. 13)

T f   61. When executing the pivot instep kick, the forward swing of the kicking leg is initiated in the hip.   (p. 18)

t F   62. When executing the throw-in, you may use one hand to throw the ball so long as the ball is delivered from over the head.   (p. 13)

T f   63. When executing the outside of the foot dribble, the ball is dribbled with the same foot every other step.   (p. 19)

t F   64. The sole of the foot and heel kicks are easier to perform if the ball is rolling and you are running.   (p. 19)

t F   65. In order to head the ball effectively, it is important to wait for the ball with both feet firmly placed on the ground.   (p. 15)

T f   66. Practice of correct movements is basic to learning soccer skills, but perfection depends upon more than mere repetition.   (p. 23)

t F   67. When charging, you must hold your arms away from the body and have both feet on the ground.   (p. 16)

T f   68. Two dangerous situations which fullbacks should avoid are dribbling and passing in front of the goal.   (p. 38)

T f   69. The center forward is primarily an offensive player.   (p. 40)

t F   70. On defense, the center half marks the opposing center half.   (p. 38)

T f   71. An important point concerning throw-in plays is to throw the ball to the feet of all teammates except the goalkeeper.   (p. 46)

t F   72. Generally the inside forwards kick all corner kicks.   (p. 40)

t F   73. A well-devised kickoff play consists of a long kick deep into the opponent's territory.   (p. 45)

T f   74. A type of soccer called Harpaston was played by the ancient Greeks.   (p. 49)

t F   75. The first intercollegiate soccer game played in America was between Rutgers and Princeton.   (p. 49)

t F   76. The fact there are presently no professional soccer leagues in the United States is the main reason for lack of interest and enthusiasm in the game.   (p. 50)

t   F   77. The attacking team can score a goal by using any portion of the arms from the elbow to the shoulder. (p. 55)

T   f   78. Within the United States, soccer's most coveted award is the National Open Challenge Cup. (p. 50)

T   f   79. Basically, the offside rule eliminates the possibility of a player remaining close to the goal area where he can score a goal from short range. (p. 55)

T   f   80. When a penalty kick has been awarded, the goalkeeper must stand stationary on the goal line until the ball is kicked. (p. 58)

t   F   81. The touchline is the line which divides the field into two equal halves. (p. 52)

T   f   82. The round-robin type of tournament is popular in a great many American schools and colleges. (p. 65)

t   F   83. Even though the sliding tackle forces the tackler to the ground, beginning players should master this skill as quickly as possible. (p. 21)

t   F   84. The fact that soccer is a team game makes it impractical for two or three students to practice game skills and strategies. (p. 28)

T   f   85. Students participating in the game of soccer must be willing to anticipate dangerous situations that can lead to injury. (p. 33)

COMPLETION

86. To kick a fast, low-curved ball with sideward spin you would use the *(outside)* of the foot kick. (p. 5)

87. The volley kick will yield a *(lofting—or a synonym)* ball, while the half-volley will produce a *(low)* ball. (p. 6)

88. A *(trap)* is considered successful when you have intercepted the ball and are ready to play it. (p. 8)

89. The only player who would not use the side of the foot trap is the *(goalkeeper)*. (p. 9)

90. The type of dribble which gives best ball control is the *(inside)* of the foot dribble. (p. 12)

91. A ball which goes out of play over a touchline is put into play by means of a *(throw-in)*. (p. 52)

92. When attempting to keep your body between an opponent and the ball, you should use the *(outside)* of the foot dribble. (p. 19)

93. To head the ball forward, the ball should make contact with the *(forehead or hairline)*. (p. 15)

94. To improve retention, it is important to learn not only the how of motor skills but also the *(why)* and *(when)*. (p. 23)

95. The primary position of play for the goalie is the *(penalty area)*. (p. 36)

96. The most successful way for the goalkeeper to clear the ball is to *(throw)* it. (p. 37)

97. Two of the most useful kicks for fullbacks are the *(volley)* and *(half-volley)*. (p. 37)

98. When a halfback marks an approaching dribbler, he should force him to the *(outside)* of the field. (p. 39)

99. When the goal kick is taken from your own goal, the *(goalkeeper)* generally kicks the ball. (p. 46)

100. The *(zone)* type of defense is recommended for beginning players since it stresses positional play. (p. 47)

101. In the three-back system, the loss of the center halfback will *(increase)* the area to be covered by the other halfbacks. (p. 42)

102. When the referee holds the ball and lets it fall to the ground between two opponents, it is called a *(drop ball)*. (p. 51)

103. Major infractions of rules and personal misconduct are offenses for which a *(direct)* free kick is given. (p. 56)

104. The *(halfback)* should develop accuracy in throwing the ball since he is usually responsible for throw-ins. (p. 39)

105. When an offensive player kicks the ball over the goal line, but fails to score a goal, a *(goal)* kick is awarded. (p. 59)

106. The side of the foot volley is used when the ball is approximately *(knee)* high or lower. (p. 20)

107. The only way to increase strength and endurance is by means of the *(overload) principle)*. (p. 30)

108. The three-back system is an effective defense against the *(W)* offense. (p. 42)

109. The four-back game utilizes one of the *(wing halfbacks)* as the fourth fullback. (p. 43)

ANSWERS TO EVALUATION QUESTIONS

*No answer

Page	Answer and Page Reference
5	*Self-testing item
6	*Self-testing item
8	*Self-testing item
10	*Self-testing item
12	*Self-testing item
13	*Self-testing item
14	*Self-testing item
16	*Self-testing item
19	*Self-testing item
20	A is in the best position; C too could tackle well but not B (who might run into the dribbler head-on and make an illegal charge; A could tackle if not running at high speed). The dribbler might evade by feinting; by passing to a teammate.
24	*Self-testing item
25	*Self-testing item
28	*Self-testing item
30	*Self-testing item
36	X should kick the ball downfield or toward the sideline, never across the goal area. Y should be prepared to guard the goal and Z should mark opposing center forward or move toward the point where the ball is directed by X.

42   It would be best for the defending team to send this throw-in to B because he is in position to move down the field. The ball should not be thrown to A for it is unwise to pass in front of the goal. A throw-in to the goalkeeper, if he is free, could be a wise move in some circumstances.

43   The goalkeeper may catch the ball and then clear it. If the throw-in is to a fullback, he may not use his hands. If the throw-in is directed to the goalkeeper, it is best to throw the ball so he can catch it.

44   B is not in good position to receive the ball; A did not "lead the receiver" (pass ball downfield in front of him); A has passed to a guarded teammate.

45   If X_2 is the goalkeeper and he is free to do so, he should move to one side of the goal area and clear the ball with either a long accurate throw or a long hard kick. A_1 should follow up his shot into the goal area. Y_2 should be ready to move in to goal area if needed there, and Z_2 should move out ready to receive pass from X_2 or play of Y_2 and Z_2 may be reversed.

46   Best strategy would be to attack in depth or waves so that the attack can be varied and a lost ball can be retrieved more easily. B and D could drop back behind C to form either a W formation or a spearhead formation. A and E should not converge toward center of field since this would close the formation and pull them out of position. It is better to carry the attack on a wide front.

56   The ball is in play. A player outside the playing area may play the ball provided it is inside the field of play.

57   Neither A nor B is offside. There were two opponents nearer the goal than A when he played the ball. B is not offside because before he played the ball it was touched by his opponent, X_2.

59   If Y is the goalkeeper, no foul has occurred. If Y is any other member of the defending team, a foul has been committed and a penalty kick is awarded the offense.

Index